SCOTLAND'S
TURNTABLE FERRIES

ROBERT BEALE & JOHN HENDY

Ferry
Publications

First published in the
Isle of Man in 2013 by
Ferry Publications
PO Box 33
Ramsey
Isle of Man IM99 4LP

CONTENTS

STROME FERRY
250 YARDS AHEAD
CAUTION

FOREWORD

By the Rt Hon Alex Salmond PC MSP

It has been my immense pleasure to make the short sea crossing to Skye, from Glenelg to Kylerhea, on the *Glenachulish*, a vessel now advancing in years but proud of her distinction as the last turntable ferry in Scotland still providing a scheduled vehicle and passenger service.

This fascinating book tells the story of Scotland's turntable ferries: the ships themselves, the routes they served, the people who sailed them and the people who sailed on them. It is full of fact, incident and anecdote. The story is told not just in words but through an impressive array of period photographs.

The growth of road transport in the twentieth century, linked to the increasing flow of visitors to the Highlands and Islands of Scotland, presented the traditional ferries, designed primarily for people and portable goods, with a new challenge. The turntable ferry was an early but lasting response to the basic challenge which faces ferry operators to this day: how to transfer vehicles between the fixed height of land with the variable height of a boat, which is rising and falling with the tide? The turntable ferry was a Scottish invention – a "simple and ingenious one" as John MacLeod says in his Introduction.

I am pleased to note that Scottish ingenuity in ferry design lives on. In December 2012, Nicola Sturgeon, Deputy First Minister for Scotland, launched the world's first seagoing roll-on roll-off hybrid ferry, the MV *Hallaig*, built by Ferguson's of Port Glasgow. She will sail on the route between Sconser in Skye and Raasay, opening up the enticing prospect for the traveller of experiencing the best of the old and the best of the new on one visit to Skye.

But this is more than just a book about ferries. It evokes the spirit of the Scottish Highlands, its people and its culture, as vibrant today as it was in past centuries. It sheds insights into the development of travel into and around the region as the motor car, gradually at first and then with increasing pace, came to dominate transport.

The *Glenachulish* is now a sprightly 44 years old and I hope we will see her in active service for many years ahead. This aim will be assisted by the generous decision of the authors to donate any profits to the *Glenachulish* Preservation Trust. I hope that reading this book will encourage many more to take a trip to Glenelg or Kylerhea and enjoy the brief but memorable experience of a sail on the *Glenachulish*.

When the time does come for this noble craft, the last of her line, to enjoy her retirement, we can be grateful to Robert Beale and John Hendy for leaving us with this lovingly-compiled archive of words and pictures to celebrate a notable Scottish invention.

INTRODUCTION

'I have regretted the passing of the Ballachulish ferry,' mused historian John Prebble in 1982, 'and others elsewhere in the Highlands, as men may once have been saddened by the loss of the old oared boats they replaced. A rocking passage across a sea-loch, enclosed in the capsule of a car, added much to the pleasures of travel, the wide sweep against the pull of the tide, the throb and smell of complaining engines, the ring of falling platforms echoing against the hills...'

The turntable ferries of the straits and sea lochs of Highland Scotland, which Prebble loved so well, are all but gone. Only the doughty little *Glenachulish* survives on her seasonal service at Kylerhea – with occasional heroism at Strome – and we should here pay tribute to those who, back in 2004, had faith in her, overcame a host of difficulties and discouragements, and have kept her in service ever since.

My own passion for these tough wee craft – exclusive to the Highlands and, indeed, a Highland invention – is largely an accident of birth. When I first drew breath, in April 1966, my father was the very young Free Church minister of Kilmallie and Arisaig – that is, western Lochaber; he kept services at minor western stations (Kinlochiel, Blaich and Trislaig) but his main pastoral responsibility was for the people of Corpach and Caol. My earliest memories, then, include jaunts by the busy ferries at Corran and Ballachulish. But the Free Church was besides something of a family business and three reverend uncles had charges, respectively, in Snizort (Skye), Scalpay (Harris) and Lochcarron. So I have vivid memories of all these turntable ferries besides, including the two Skye crossings: their gay colours and their soft-spoken and

Over forty years after the Strome ferry closed, in January 2012 a rock fall on the road that replaced it necessitated a brief ferry revival using the surviving *Glenachulish*. She is seen arriving at North Strome. *(Stevie Watson)*

ineffably calm skippers and crew; the eerie swing of the vehicle-deck – you always feared it might catch on something but it never did; the *whumph* of ramp on concrete, the *du-dump* as each car boarded. The boil from the screws and the surge of the wake, the pulse of engines and the scent of the sea...

We do not know, and cannot now ascertain, the name of the man at Ballachulish who, just before the Great War, invented the turntable ferry. But the concept was simple and ingenious. It allowed, in its earliest form, the adaptation of really quite a traditional boat – the beamy Highland coble – to side-load a car from a stone or concrete slipway and at any state of the tide; even better for the intrepid motorist of the day, he at no point needed to reverse. We would go on building turntable ferries for six decades more and, by 1960, they were large and sophisticated craft: the fine vessels latterly built for the Kyleakin crossing, for instance, had two big Gleniffer engines, twin-screw propulsion, a roomy saloon for passengers (complete with padded leather seating) and comfortable capacity for six cars. The last vessel for the narrows of Loch Carron, the 1962 *Pride of Strome*, was another powerful beauty of a boat and the last turntable ferry ever built – the 1973 *Lochaber* – reached the boundaries of the turntable principle, with her lofty A-framing, mighty engines and room for nine big cars. She was vast. She was magnificent. But, even then, she was an anachronism and her huge vehicle deck was so difficult for men to turn when fully laden, that machinery had subsequently to be installed to do it for them.

Turntable ferries had contributed enormously to the ease and expansion of post-war motor tourism and, off-season, remained important links in an old Highland economy. (To the very end, in 1975, the wonderful tariff-boards by the slips of Ballachulish specified fares in near-numbing detail: 35p for a car; up to 75p for a van or lorry; a bicycle at a generous 4p but a bob for a tandem; 20p for a horse and cart; tuppence for a sheep; 80p for a stirk and a gulping 10p for 'Cows and Two Year Olds...' Which – in a nice instance of dry Highland humour – reminds me of a good Prebble anecdote of the Ballachulish crossing. In latter decades the chief of Clan Cameron – The Lochiel himself, as laird of the Lochaber side – was, among

other baubles and distinctions, hereditary Chairman of the Ballachulish Ferry Co. Ltd, 'and it was the gentle custom of some habitual travellers,' Prebble remembered, 'to grumble at him when the fares rose yet again. On a grey spring morning, with rain strung like fine wire from sky to loch, the ticket-seller tapped at my car window, a white face bending in an oilskin cap. I paid the fare and added a blessing upon Lochiel. "Aye," said she in understanding, "if he had charged like this at Culloden, he would have won..."

By the mid 1960s, though, it was evident that where there was no convenient detour by road and where demand for passage was high – most notoriously at Strome and Kyleakin – these little boats, working as they might, simply could not handle vast numbers of cars. And the sheer, ballooning, implacable expansion of car use and Highland motoring holidays caught everyone by surprise. At the end of 1954, Lochiel and his colleagues were undoubtedly startled to note that, through the year, they had conveyed 42,000 cars over the Narrows. In 1974 – with the new bridge already rising – they would carry 204,000; and that was with an alternative 19-mile road round by Loch Leven, generally quicker if your wait for ferry passage would be more than half an hour. At Strome, the only alternative was a gulping 140-mile detour – and the queues even by the mid 1950s were appalling.

The other difficulty was that, by nature of the design – a revolving vehicle-deck on a central bearing – a turntable ferry could not carry any single vehicle much heavier than nine metric tons; nor could any carry the longest vehicles allowed on British roads by the 1970s. That was not much of a concern when heavy goods, coal and so on was largely conveyed directly to West Highland communities by little puffers and MacBrayne cargo-boats – or at least freighted by rail to the likes of Mallaig and Kyle. From the early 1950s, though, there was a remorseless and – as it proved – irreversible shift to haulage by road, especially after the advent of the first big MacBrayne car ferries, in the Hebrides, in 1964.

There were besides, perhaps – especially after dreadful accidents at Kylesku and Kyleakin in the late fifties, drowning between them seven people – new concerns about the safety of the design. (It is not a

Opposite: The *Glenachulish* is seen in her normal environment as she approaches the Glenelg slipway in August 2012. (*John Hendy*)

concern now; when I stupidly loosed my handbrake seconds too soon on the *Glenachulish* last January, as she took the slip at North Strome – and it is a phenomenon of that ferry that, when full-astern power is applied, her bows always rise – I had the brief and extraordinary sense that she was going one way and the jetty and onlookers were going another, before my Ford Focus, hurtling backwards, hit the port rear ramp with an enormous bang. But - secured by spring-bracing, a latch, and a securely looped chain – it did not fail, nor was anything (including my bumper) damaged, though there was great hilarity on shore at my expense and the skipper – the sturdy Quentin 'Q' Banting, of distinguished career in the Royal Navy and who once enjoyed battle-command in the US Fleet during the first Gulf War – emerged to howl theatrically, 'I thought he was going to come through the wheelhouse!' He had every right to be angry: had that ramp not held, I might well have killed him.

So they began to disappear, the little turntable ferries; and when they went, they went very quickly. In 1966, seventeen were still in passenger service – one at Cuan, one at Bonawe, three at Ballachulish, two at Corran, one at Kessock, one at Kylerhea, three at Kyleakin, two at Strome, two at Kylesku and one at Scalpay. By 1976, there were only seven – the *Gleann Mhor* and the *Lochaber* at Corran; the *Glenachulish* (deployed largely as the back-up ferry at Kessock), the *The Maid of Kylesku* and the *Queen of Kylesku* on the Sutherland passage, the second *Scalpay* on the Harris station and the *Glen Mallie* at Kylerhea. By 1986, there was only the *Glenachulish*; and long may she sail. She is perfectly suited for the conditions and traffic offering on what, these days, is marketed primarily as a charming tourist experience.

A turntable ferry could have served Scalpay perfectly well until the 1997 advent of her bridge and one would still be perfectly appropriate for Luing. But, by the mid 1970s, Kylesku trade was increasingly beyond them and although the *Gleann Mhor* and the *Lochaber* were still perfectly on top of things at Corran when superseded by large, redundant corner-loaders – first from Kessock; then Kylesku – turntable ferries could not manage the weight and number of vehicles seeking passage now, three decades later.

But perhaps the biggest compliment we could pay these craft is that of all the routes they ever served – and the story of each of these eleven is here, in this excellent account, related in close detail – only three have a car ferry service today (and that at Kylerhea, of course, is still operated by a turntable vessel.) On all the others – Strome being a sad exception, a seasonal service could still profitably cross these straits of Loch Carron – the supposedly bigger and better craft all in time failed, and characterless bridges vault the waters in their stead.

We should also, of course, remember operators and crew. One or two of the services detailed here were not noted for shrewd management, brave vision or evident professionalism. They were the exception. The long service of John MacAllistair as ferryman of Luing is here recorded and the remarkable Buchanans and Mackintoshes of Ardgour ran the Corran service, to a high standard, for many years. Murdo MacKenzie – still, happily, spared, in patriarchal old age – with scant capital, no support from public funds and through many discouragements revived the Kylerhea crossing to Skye, kept it going through over thirty years, and handed on a service with sufficient fame and goodwill to continue ever since. The MacSweens of Scalpay were universally respected, within that little island and

The *Lochalsh* (II) unloading at Kyleakin.

The Corran ferry **Maid of Glengour** is somewhat dominated by the massif of Ben Keil as she approaches Nether Lochaber with a single car.

beyond, and – whatever you think of lairds and clan chiefs – both Lochiels fought bravely for this country in respective, terrible wars, and presided, in turn, over a very efficient and happy Ballachulish crossing; Donald, XXVth of Lochiel, and his colleagues finally yielded to the hideous 1975 bridge with signal grace.

As for the men who physically worked these vessels – and most, well into the 1950s, without as much as the scantiest covered wheelhouse and through the best and worst of Highland weather – they are everywhere affectionately recalled. Recently a current member of the Corran ferry crew, Steven Munro – whose people have a long association with that crossing – forwarded me a 1981 note from an English clergyman (who had long made annual holiday in Ardgour) to his grandfather, and which may have been a sermon or radio-broadcast.

"It was an August morning. The sun had risen high above the Ardgour hills, and now shone with a brilliance that would have raised the dullest of spirits. I stood on the slipway, gazing across the narrows of Loch Linnhe, awaiting the return of the Corran ferry as she swung back into the tide. Behind me lay a dozen cars where the world had come to rest and where time lapped pleasantly upon the ebb.

On the opposite shore, breathing their familiar welcome, stood the lighthouse, and to the right, the homely outline of the Ardgour Hotel, its whitened walls drenched in the morning sun. The approaching chug of the ferry sent me back to my car. I was among the first six vehicles, and so would make the crossing without further wait – a mixed blessing since I was loathe to terminate the pure pleasure and luxury of the present scene.

There is an atmosphere about these Highland ferries that casts the mind back into the simplicities of the past, and one becomes jealous for their survival. Certainly they have advanced, like many other things with the passing of time, and no longer present the challenge and hazard of former days when great care was required in driving the car onto much smaller ferries. But for all that, they still retain that fascinating link with all that is lovely of Highland life. They provide the car driver with that valuable opportunity and enforced discipline of leaving the car, to stand still and absorb, to open the heart to that deeper penetration of beauty. How much we have lost in the erection of that new bridge at Ballachulish, and how much have we gained? This is a question each one must answer for himself. Perhaps we should be thankful for both, so long as both are permitted to remain.

Corran Ferry will always remain with particular affection for me, since over the years there has developed a regard and a friendship for one of the ferrymen who is pleased to recognise me from year to year, and who shares his warm greetings and conversation during the brief crossing, reminding me that the strongest ties of life's pleasures are not so much bound up in things and places, as in human relationships and affection. Ballachulish Bridge may well cut an hour off one's travels, but the cold iron of its girders can never compensate for the warmth of the ferryman's smile.

I have often thought about him, plying his small craft backwards and forwards with monotonous regularity from sunrise to sundown, day in and day out. What does he achieve in life? His task offers no sense of achievement. There is no journey that leads to a destination, but a continual undoing of all that has been done. He may be a father, I thought, or a husband, whose only satisfaction on returning home is the remembrance of the many journeys which have done nothing more than return him to the place where he started. But like the pendulum that never ceases to swing, the degree of blessing will only be measured by those who stop to look at the hands that move. So with my ferryman. He will never know how many travellers he has helped on their way, or the wealth of his smiles to the strangers who can never forget."

Though very pretty – they were usually painted in bright hues, and it is striking how many post-war colour postcards feature these vessels – the turntable ferries have never enjoyed the following of, say, the stately paddlers and turbine steamers of the Clyde, or even some of the early, major car ferries and the last of the MacBrayne mail boats, such the handsome but – even at her launch – obsolete *Claymore* of 1955.

Robert Beale and John Hendy are to be congratulated for enterprising a book long overdue, scrupulously researched and beautifully illustrated.

The *Queen of Kylesku*.
(Dave Hewitt)

The *Glencoe* (II) crosses the narrows at Ballachulish.

The project has involved both men in long hours of toil, the checking and re-checking of facts and some daunting physical travel: Robert, for instance, made two arduous day-trips from Cumbria to Lochaber to consult the records of the Ballachulish Ferry Co. Ltd. They have gone to great length to unearth original and striking photographs, many here published for the first time. They have spent precious time besides in direct correspondence or interview with surviving skippers, managers and crew. Company records will be around for decades to come; the old ferrymen will not. Much is here recorded which might otherwise have been, within a few years, lost forever.

Both authors would join me besides in acknowledging the honour the Rt Hon. Alex Salmond PC MSP has done them and reader alike in taking the time to contribute his charming Foreword. I have known the First Minister for over quarter of a century.

That relationship has been inevitably strained, at times, by our respective trades; as H L Mencken famously put it, the proper relationship of any journalist to any politician is that of a dog to a lamp post. But I have never, on any meeting with the man, found him anything less than straightforward and genial. And there is a depth of love for his country – and for the small things, quiet trades and toiling people of his country – in the First Minister that few have a chance to see. I know that he and Mrs Salmond are frequent travellers, on vacation, by the waters of Kylerhea; and how much their annual visits and cheerful interest in the *Glenachulish*, her management and crew, mean to all concerned.

John MacLeod,
Marybank,
Isle of Lewis.

THE TURNTABLE FERRIES OF SCOTLAND

The manually operated turntable ferry was a peculiarly Scottish phenomenon. Their introduction and development mirrors the growth of car ownership and the ability of the more wealthy and adventurous minority to explore the beautiful and remoter corners of the western Highlands.

Although many of the crossings were eventually to host a turntable ferry, the services had been operated by a succession of larger rowing or sailing boats for centuries, some to islands – there were two traditional short crossings to Skye – but most over the narrows of assorted 'sea lochs'; the long, tidal inlets unique to the West Highlands. This made travel by land difficult - often with extended detours inland - to do what, as the seagull flies, is a very short distance. (Indeed, we readily forget that well within living memory most freight – and many tourists – sailed direct to the Hebrides from Glasgow; and that MacBrayne's last cargo-boat, the *Lochcarron*, only quit her Glasgow-Stornoway duties in 1976.) The little ferries, for the more local and the most intrepid, crossed these straits and reduced travelling time.

Industry in the seventeenth and eighteenth centuries boosted these crossings and with the increase of the cattle trade, the drove roads and ferries became well used – though cattle in large numbers were usually swum across. Kelp – seaweed harvested and burned for potash, used in the manufacture of glass and soap – was briefly important during the Napoleonic Wars. The coming of the Royal Mail kept ferries all the busier; at Corran, there were timetabled crossings for the post in Victoria's long reign. People taking them would have been largely locals and those on business; tourism was still in its infancy - and very expensive. That said, some notable gentry did mention the small ferries in their writings such as Johnson and Boswell, Lord Cockburn or Dorothy Wordsworth, who crossed at Bonawe and Shian. She was impressed by the ability of the "lad" operating the boat at Bonawe but thought the ferryman's house at Shian was "dirty" and full of "wretchedly dirty children"!

The arrival of paddle steamers and, late in the Victorian era, Highland steam trains made travel to the north-west quick and affordable. Tourism was no longer the prerogative of the rich. Circular tours were introduced throughout the Clyde and Western Isles opening people's eyes to the grandeur of the country.

When vehicles on the road became more than just experiments, the internal combustion engine became real competition for the old steamer routes – where roads existed. In the years after the Great War, the small ferries became vital links in the road network. The first intrepid motorists had braved little more than barges, boarded by narrow springy planks. By the 1920s these rapidly yielded to the turntable ferries of our study. They were – and largely remained, even in much larger and more sophisticated form by the 1960s – unglamorous workhorses. And, lacking the fine lines and glamour of, say, the great Clyde steamers, they have had sadly little attention.

The earliest home-spun ferries were fraught. Cars were stowed at right angles which certainly caused stability problems and accidents were not infrequent. Gently sloping slipways or jetties were constructed in order to allow vessels to come alongside at any state of the tide and the introduction of the turntable device at Ballachulish allowed a safer and simpler service to be offered. Vehicles could now drive on at an angle, ramps could be raised and the turntable swung in order to allow cars to drive off at the other end in the normal manner without having to reverse. It caught on. Turntable ferries became ubiquitous in the West Highlands, brought communities together, saved long inland detours and greatly eased access by new, flocking tourism.

Yet their very success would prove their undoing. During the late 1950s and early 1960s, so popular did motoring become that the small ferries on the busiest routes – most conveying no more than half a dozen cars – were swamped by the traffic on offer. The 'Glasgow Herald' (10th January 1962), states that in 1950 the ferries at Kylesku, Ballachulish and Kyleakin had carried a combined 63,000 vehicles. By 1960 the three crossings bore, between them, a gulping 302,000.

Above: The *Maid of Luing* (*Brian Maxted*)

Opposite: The construction of the new bridge was well underway in May 1974 as the *Glen Duror* (right) and *Glenachulish* cross each other. (*David Parsons*)

At Ballachulish, the ferry company erected signs by the side of the queuing lanes informing advancing motorists how long they would have to wait until crossing the narrows of Loch Leven. If stopping adjacent to the 'Half Hour' sign it was usually quicker to drive around via Kinlochleven – a 19-mile detour. It was not simply volumes of traffic that left the turntable ferries wanting but also their inability to carry increasingly long and heavy loads. On the main Kyleakin crossing to Skye, and from the mid 1960s, the Caledonian Steam Packet Co.Ltd declined to build further turntable craft, instead experimenting with a fixed-ramp side-loading design. Though three were built, these proved – if anything – even less efficient. The future, with the advent of the Scottish Transport Group in 1969, lay with modern and much larger double-ended ferries, able to carry many cars at a time and the heaviest vehicles allowed on British roads; and besides a new generation of 'Small Island Class' bow loaders, which provided assorted small Hebrides with their first car ferry service or developed 'back door' crossings to larger islands like Arran and Mull. (These little craft are themselves now obsolete, having yielded almost everywhere to double-ended 'Loch Class' vessels.)

In the early 1960s, frustrations boiled over in the particular case of Strome, where the crossing was the only alternative to an enormous detour and where it was evident that – in high summer and even with new and bigger boats – the service could not cope. Questions were even asked in Parliament. And as early as 1935, the House of Commons had its attention drawn to "unsatisfactory and irregular" service across Kylesku in northwest Sutherland while a bridge was proposed, half a century before it happened. By the late 1960s, the Kyleakin crossing was choking on summer traffic, even with four boats running simultaneously and two loading-berths on either side.

So larger boats came and roads were improved; in time, bridges spanned Ballachulish, Kessock, Kylesku and Kyleakin and the little turntable ferries faded from the Highland scene. What had once been a common sight in Gaeldom lives today in just one ship at one last crossing: the sturdy, Clyde-built *Glenachulish* on her summer trade at Kylerhea. She is now, belatedly cherished as part of Scotland's national heritage.

We here detail the history of the vessels and the routes on which they traded. They were generally held as lowly craft – a prosaic part of the road network; records are mean and little regard has been paid them in the many books, over many decades, honouring (for instance) the mail boats of MacBrayne or the summer-butterfly paddlers and turbine steamers of the Clyde. Assembling, for the first time, a historic record of the Highland turntable ferries and the routes they operated has not been easy. But we here bring together as much information as is available - all in one place for the first time.

Robert Beale   John Hendy
Kendal   Romney Marsh
Cumbria   Kent
                                             March 2013

Right and opposite: The pioneer turntable ferry was the **Glencoe** (I) of 1912 which is seen here undergoing her stability trials. Today's Health & Safety Executive would certainly not have approved. *(both Brian Maxted collection)*

THE FERRY CROSSINGS

BALLACHULISH – Loch Leven (South Ballachulish to North Ballachulish on A82)

The name Ballachulish is of course, Gaelic, and means 'Little Township on the Narrows'. It is a large, pleasant village on the south shore of Loch Leven, a mile or so to the east of the straits proper and which until very near the end of the final closure of the ferry in 1975, was dominated by its slate-quarries and disfiguring heaps of spoil.

Loch Leven forms the natural border between the old Argyll and Inverness County Councils and should not be confused with the loch of the same name on the other side of the country, between Kinross and Fife which bears an island fastness in which Mary, Queen of Scots was briefly imprisoned. But it has islands of its own, notably Eilean Munde, with its ruinous chapel and the historic burial ground of the MacDonalds of Glencoe, the Stewarts of Ballachulish and the Camerons of Callart which was chosen for their dead, one suspects, because wolves could not reach it. (It would be the eighteenth century before Scotland's last were exterminated.)

The historic Ballachulish crossing – and it is ancient – was significantly to the east of that which, from 1912, boasted a car ferry service. In fact, there were three widely used routes, including passage from Invercoe to Callert and from Caolas na Con, the latter east of Ballachulish village itself. And that old Ballachulish ferry plays its part in the tales of a very dark period in Highland history, most infamously the Massacre of Glencoe, in February 1692. When Lieutenant-Colonel James Hamilton received the order to massacre the Macdonalds of Glencoe, he was waiting by the Ballachulish ferry. The crew were ordered to remain on the south side so a quick escape could be made to Fort William and a guard was stationed there to make sure that they did.

No less bitterly recalled is the Appin Murder. On 14th May 1752, six years after the battle of Culloden, Colin Campbell, a detested local official in an area

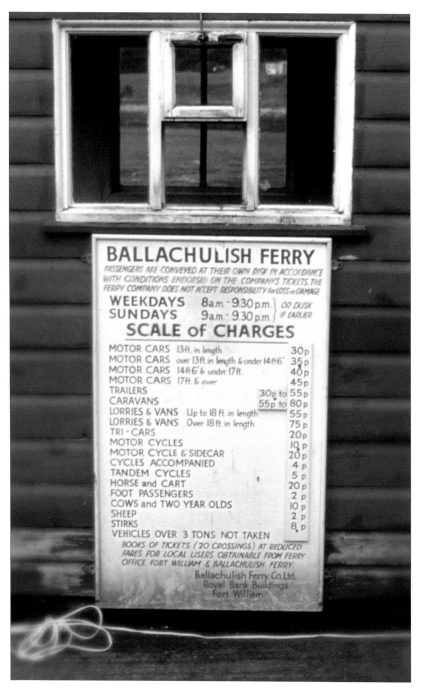

BALLACHULISH FERRY

PASSENGERS ARE CONVEYED AT THEIR OWN RISK IN ACCORDANCE WITH CONDITIONS ENDORSED ON THE COMPANY'S TICKETS. THE FERRY COMPANY DOES NOT ACCEPT RESPONSIBILITY for LOSS or DAMAGE

WEEKDAYS   8 a.m - 9.30 p.m.⎱ OR DUSK
SUNDAYS   9 a.m - 9.30 p.m.⎰ IF EARLIER

SCALE of CHARGES

MOTOR CARS	13 ft. in length	30 p
MOTOR CARS	over 13 ft. in length & under 14 ft 6"	35 p
MOTOR CARS	14 ft 6' & under 17 ft.	40 p
MOTOR CARS	17 ft. & over	45 p
TRAILERS		30 p to 55 p
CARAVANS		55 p to 80 p
LORRIES & VANS	Up to 18 ft. in length	55 p
LORRIES & VANS	Over 18 ft. in length	75 p
TRI - CARS		20 p
MOTOR CYCLES		10 p
MOTOR CYCLE & SIDECAR		20 p
CYCLES ACCOMPANIED		4 p
TANDEM CYCLES		5 p
HORSE and CART		20 p
FOOT PASSENGERS		2 p
COWS and TWO YEAR OLDS		10 p
SHEEP		2 p
STIRKS		8 p
VEHICLES OVER 3 TONS NOT TAKEN		

BOOKS OF TICKETS (20 CROSSINGS) AT REDUCED FARES FOR LOCAL USERS OBTAINABLE FROM FERRY OFFICE FORT WILLIAM & BALLACHULISH FERRY.

Ballachulish Ferry Co.Ltd.
Royal Bank Buildings.
Fort William.

practically under military occupation and dubbed contemptuously *Am Madadh Ruadha* (the 'Red Fox'), was fatally shot after crossing the ferry from the Lochaber side. The assassin was glimpsed fleeing into the woods. Campbell was the prosperous factor of a few small local estates declared forfeit after their lairds had 'come out' on Prince Charlie's side at the Rising of 1745. Campbells generally were unpopular in this district and many people had a motive specifically to kill the 'Red Fox'; but what followed was cynical and more convenient than convincing. After but two days James Stewart was arrested and brought to trial. With

eleven of the fifteen jurors being Campbells, and with outrageous and evident bias by judge and official, he was convicted, condemned, and in short order hanged, atop a crag just south of Caolas Mhic Phadraig, the tightest straits of Loch Leven. Afterwards, the rotting corpse was hung high in a gibbet as a warning to others and when the skeleton disintegrated the bones were simply restrung. The name of the real murderer is still known in the oldest families of Appin, Ardgour and Duror but kept as a hereditary secret.

Terror passed; the first, intrepid tourists began to explore. James Lettice travelling in 1792 complained that the boat at Ballachulish was too small to convey a carriage with its horses and passengers in one trip. In the early eighteenth century new quays were constructed after a survey was completed by Thomas Telford and James Hope.

From 1903 until its closure at Easter 1966, Ballachulish boasted a railway service as a spur (from Connel) of the Callander & Oban Railway; happy Edwardian plans for further extension, by bridge, to Fort William were never achieved, far less the ultimate dream of a Great Glen run through to Inverness. In fact the district enjoyed two stations; Ballachulish proper, in the village and as terminus which was signposted 'for Glen Coe and Kinlochleven', and Ballachulish Ferry as penultimate halt. But it would be 1927 before a road ran either side of Loch Leven to Kinlochleven – a community erected only, at the turn of the century, by a new industry and which narrowly escaped being named Aluminiumville – and for over two decades David MacBrayne Ltd ran a direct passenger vessel service from Ballachulish to

Kinlochleven, linking dams and plant and management to the railhead and the south.

By the Great War, though, and with the advent of both motor-powered vessels and a handy railway station and a respectable road to the north by Nether Lochaber to Fort William, Ballachulish ferry proper crossed at Caolas Mhic Phadraig, the 'Straits of the son of Peter'. Loch Leven here is at its narrowest - in still, favourable conditions you can readily stand on one side and conduct a coherent if loud conversation with someone on the other; but the tide-race here, especially on the ebb, is considerable.

The first car was carried in 1906 on an extremely basic vessel which was operated by the proprietor of the Ballachulish Hotel (doing very nicely out of the new railway link.) She carried one car which was loaded by means of planks so that the vehicle was 'parked' at right angles to the vessel.

1906 also saw the first motor bus connect with the ferry, introduced by the recently re-structured MacBraynes. At first it ran between Fort William and North Ballachulish but was extended through to Kinlochleven after the construction of the road. The vehicle was a 14-seat chain driven Albion which was scheduled to connect with the trains departing from Ballachulish Ferry station to Oban. Ample time was given for the ferry crossing.

The early history of the Ballachulish turntable ferries is difficult to ascertain. It is known that the first turntable vessel to operate at Ballachulish was the *Glencoe* (I) of 1912 which was also the first turntable ferry ever built. She was constructed on the Gareloch at Clynder and delivered to Ballachulish in July 1912. She could carry a truck, as she did on her trials, but usually just conveyed one motor car at a time across Loch Leven. Mary Weir, in her book 'Ferries in Scotland' states that a second vessel of similar design entered service along with the *Glencoe* (I). This statement may well be true as an early picture shows two similar turntable ferries at Ballachulish but this could just be an image from the late 1920s when a new vessel was introduced.

For 15 years, of course, the ferry was the only way for cars to proceed north from Ballachulish, as there was no road around the head of the loch until 1927. Following its construction, the ferry saved a 19-mile

detour on the coastal highway round Loch Leven but in high summer in the final years of the crossing the road was a useful safety-valve for impatient motorists and prevented the sort of seething tourist log-jam that latterly beset Kyleakin, Strome and Kylesku.

The year 1926 saw the arrival of the *Glencoe* (II) which was built to a similar design to the *Glencoe* (I). It was in the early 1930s that a proposal was put forward to build a transporter bridge across Loch Leven, as had already been done at Middlesbrough, Teeside, but nothing ever came of it. It will be seen

Opposite: (left) The Scale of Charges at Ballachulish Ferry was very detailed and catered for every eventuality. (Helmut Zozmann)

Left: How things used to be done as a Daimler is loaded via planks onto an early Ballachulsh ferry. There was not much margin for error. (Scottish Motor Museum Trust)

*Below: The **Maid of Glencoe** (I) was the third turntable ferry at Ballachulish and entered service in 1935.*

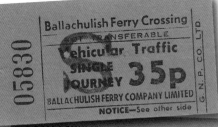

that between 1926 and 1935, there were two vessels operating with the same name. As the second *Glencoe* was originally built to replace the earlier ship and at that time boats of this size did not require registration with the Board of Trade, they were usually referred to as the '1' and the '2'.

A 1920s photograph has recently surfaced showing the *Glencoe* (I) at the Ardgour slipway, now part of the Corran ferry - unloading an ambulance a decade before the vehicle service started there. It is probable that if the price was right a Ballachulish ferry would on occasion convey vehicles to the crude slip at Ardgour to save the long and rough drive around the head of Loch Eil. But the need for a regular car ferry at Corran was growing evident.

In 1935 the Ballachulish Ferry Company Ltd was formed, taking over from the Ballachulish Hotel. The company was an equal partnership between the Lochiel and Ballachulish estates, they being the major landowners on each side of the ferry. The manager of the Ballachulish Ferry Co. Ltd. was Robert H MacQueen and a perk of the job – for MacQueen and his successors – was the tied accommodation, the old and stately Ballachulish House. From this period onwards, besides, we have a detailed and accurate historic record – the Company papers survive, and can be consulted by the general public at Fort William's Lochaber Archive Centre.

The first new vessel was the *Maid of Glencoe* (I) which appeared in 1935, built by Hugh MacLean & Sons Ltd of Renfrew. Her arrival led to the withdrawal of the *Glencoe* (I) which was sold on for use at Corran. The new wooden craft carried two cars and although in appearance she was an unremarkable vessel, she worked well enough for a sister to be built which was the *Queen of Glen Albyn*, introduced in 1936. She was built by the firm of Messrs Stevenson and Asher,

Above: A Ballachulish ferry ticket *(John Newth collection)*

Right: The *Glencoe* (II) is seen on a still summer's day at South Ballachulish during 1931. Note her exhaust cloud as she waits to depart.

Shipbuilders, of Banff; and her arrival allowed the disposal of the *Glencoe* (II) which followed her elder sister to Corran. The 2-car vessels reliably worked the Loch Leven crossing, along with the passenger-only launches, until the early 1950s.

In July 1936 the *Queen of Glen Albyn* was washed out to sea when her engine broke down at a critical moment as she was about to be made fast for the evening. James Clark was at the helm and was set to pass the mooring line to shipmate Archie Campbell, alongside in a rowing boat. They had a long fraught night at the mercy of tide and current. The following morning at 05.00 the *Maid of Glencoe* (I) headed out to search for the men and boats, finally finding them at Kilmalieu, nine miles away on the Ardgour coast. Understandably, no Ballachulish car ferry ran that day.

The distinctive colours of the Ballachulish boats were a green hull with a red turntable. This almost certainly reflected the clan tartan of the Company chairman – Donald Walter Cameron of Lochiel (1876-

1951), who had succeeded his father as XXIVth Chief of the Camerons in 1905 and had served with distinction in the Great War. The chiefdom – and the chairmanship! – duly passed to his son, Donald Hamish Cameron, XXVth of Lochiel (1910-2004): he had served no less doughtily in the war against Nazi Germany, and sat on all sorts of boards and held all sorts of offices, notably as Kilmallie's representative on Inverness County Council and, from 1971 to 1985, as Lord Lieutenant of the County.

The minutes of the Ballachulish Ferry Co. Ltd. report many diverting problems. One was jellyfish. Loch Leven swarmed with them, especially at Caolas Mhic

Above: The **Mamore** was the Ballachulish Ferry Co's first post-war ferry which entered service in 1951.

Left: A tight squeeze as an American chassied Reo coach is loaded on board the **Glencoe** (II). *(Scottish Motor Museum Trust)*

Below left: The second *Glencoe* served the route for some ten years before being sold for further use at Corran. This fine study of the vessel shows the ample belting which formed added protection along her wooden hull.

Below right: The **Queen of Glen Albyn** dated from 1936 and was eventually sold for work at Kyerhea. She is seen unloading an MG. *(Scottish Motor Museum Trust)*

Phadraig. Frequently, these were sucked into the saltwater cooling-systems of the ferries and as often as not jammed them. The problem was cured on later craft, by the simple expedient of wire-grates over the intakes.

1951 saw the introduction of the *Mamore*. Heavily indebted in size and lines to a recent Corran ferry, the *Garven* of 1949, she could carry four small cars, boasted a new hull-form and had A-framed railings (rather than boards) on the turntable itself. The *Mamore* was designed (as would be all subsequent Ballachulish craft) by G L Watson & Co. of Liverpool – best known, then and now, for their yachts - and built by James Noble (Fraserburgh) Ltd, who would construct all the other Balachulish ferries save the last. Fraserburgh, too, was from now on their port of registry. Later vessels improved on the original *Mamore* design with increased length and the addition of a wheelhouse at the stern, although none ever had covered accommodation for passengers. The *Mamore* displaced no ship and was acquired to increase capacity. As built, her steering positions were exposed; later, her crew enjoyed a basic shelter, probably added after the *Appin Chief* entered service in 1955.

Also in 1951, new mooring-buoys were put in place for the larger vessels now appearing on the route. Sutherland County Council approached the Ballachulish Ferry Company, hoping to charter the *Maid of Glencoe* (I), probably for service at Kylesku.

The Company declined. That same year, *Maid of Glencoe* (I) and *Queen of Glen Albyn* were both overhauled at Inverness.

The three vehicle ferries worked together, usually with a one-boat service in winter and a two-boat service in summer. The third boat (and usually the oldest) was always kept ready for breakdown cover. Only on the rarest occasions – such as the first Saturday of Glasgow Fair Fortnight, when traffic heading north was prodigious – would all three craft run at once. The chief difficulty, as 1970s deckhand Edward Barrow recalls, is that the ferry invariably took longer to unload and load than to cross the narrow passage – and, with only two slips available, a 3-ship operation had little impact on queues.

In 1952 the Kessock Ferry Committee asked to charter a Ballachulish ferry for a 6-week period during January and February 1953 as their own vessel, the *Eilean Dubh,* would be off for overhaul. The Company had the *Maid of Glencoe* (I) surveyed to see if she was suitable for the route but- frustratingly – it is not recorded whether she ever sailed on the Inverness/Black Isle passage.

In 1953 the Ballachulish ferry was in operation from 08.00 until 20.00 during summer while in winter, services started at 09.00 and continued until dusk after which a passenger-only service was offered. The company had various launches for this, such as *Babe, Corsair, Malus* and *Mila*. At one time there were more

than six small boats available, some for hire and some for the passenger sailings. The *Corsair* offered pleasure trips along Loch Leven during the early 1950s until her sale in 1952.

1955 saw the *Appin Chief* enter service; a 4-car vessel similar to the *Mamore* but with a basic shelter for the helmsman at the stern. This was a metal framing which could be covered in canvas although a more substantial wheelhouse was later added. Her arrival meant that the *Maid of Glencoe* (I) was withdrawn; she was simply broken up on site and such spare parts squirreled away as might be of use in servicing the rest of the fleet.

The *Appin Chief* was duly joined, in 1957, by the *Maid of Glencoe* (II) another 4-car ferry – although she was a little longer, of subtly different hull-form and with a sturdy wheelhouse and also built by James Noble (Fraserburgh) Ltd. With three larger vessels now operating, the *Queen of Glen Albyn* was held in reserve until the *Maid of Glencoe* (II) had proved reliable after which the 1936 vessel was put on the market. She was sold to Murdo MacKenzie of Glenelg in 1959 and began what would prove a brief Kylerhea career in the spring of 1960.

The *Appin Chief*'s engine proved dubious and in 1958 it was decided to put the *Maid of Glencoe* (II)'s engine in the *Appin Chief* and a new engine in the younger vessel. It was probably on this occasion that the *Appin Chief* acquired her proper wheelhouse.

In 1959, the *Queen of Glen Albyn* left for Glenelg and major fleet upgrade – as summer traffic continued pitilessly to expand – shortly followed. The *Mamore* and *Appin Chief* were withdrawn, the *Mamore* being sold to Sutherland County Council for £1,200 and at last providing them with a relief vessel for Kylesku. During the previous year she had been offered to the proprietors of the Corran ferry for the same sum of £1,200 but they passed her up. The *Mamore* was retained at Kylesku until the commissioning of *Queen of Kylesku* in 1967 and saw her last service – probably as a stripped pontoon – in the extension of a Lochinver pier later that year before her hulk was finally abandoned on the shore.

The *Appin Chief* followed the *Queen of Glen Albyn* to Glenelg, sailing from Loch Leven for the Sound of Sleat on 25th April 1961.

The six car *Glen Mallie* and *Glen Duror* were introduced in 1959 and 1961 respectively, with the *Glen Duror* entering service in September. She would stay until the end of the Ballachulish service and be readily distinguished, to the last, by her all-green wheelhouse: on subsequent craft, the upper half was painted cream.

The *Glen Mallie* had been fitted with experimental aluminium ramps, which made life much easier for her crew. The *Maid of Glencoe* (II) duly acquired her own set at her next Inverness overhaul. Unfortunately, the Thornbush yard failed to change the counterweights

Above: The **Maid of Glencoe** marooned by the tide while the **Queen of Glen Albyn** maintains the ferry service. *(Falkirk Museums)*

Below left: Seen in March 1973, the four-year old **Glenachulish** was the final ferry to be built for the Ballachulish Ferry Company. *(John Hendy)*

Below right: The **Maid of Glencoe** (II) was eventually sold for further service in the Western Isles where she became the **Scalpay** (I).

and, with much lighter ramps, crew then struggled to lower them. The weights were subsequently adjusted by the British Aluminium Company at Kinlochleven.

The *Glen Duror* was fitted with an innovative hydraulic reversing gear, as opposed to the standard manual gear systems. This upgrade, though, gave nothing but trouble until in 1963 it was removed at Inverness and replaced with a manual gear. She was besides plagued with a stiff turntable – especially when fully laden - and this was rectified in the same refit by adjusting the bearings to raise it a little further from the deck.

In 1963, after inspecting the new *Pride of Strome* at Stromeferry, the Ballachulish Ferry Company invited Forbes of Sandhaven to tender for the next vessel built at Ballachulish. It is unclear if one was ever submitted and, in fact, the Forbes yard never built another turntable ferry.

In 1964 the *Glen Duror* and *Maid of Glencoe* (II) went to Inverness as usual for their overhaul, but due to the temporary closure of the Caledonian Canal (at the critical juncture) the *Glen Mallie* was overhauled at Ballachulish.

A new six-car ferry named *Glen Loy* was introduced in 1964 and would serve until the end, although like the *Glen Duror* would have much trouble with her reverse-gear and was also the last turntable ferry to be built with counterweighted ramps. The *Maid of Glencoe* (II) was then advertised for sale and was viewed by a Mr Jay Scott of Inversnaid, Loch Lomond, who took her out for trials – probably with a view to a car ferry service to Rowardennan - but he did not proceed with the purchase. Her transport overland – or, perhaps, up the River Leven - could have been excessively exciting. She was finally acquired by David MacBrayne Ltd for £1,600, refitted at Shandon on the Gareloch and inaugurated their new Scalpay-Kyles Scalpay service in May 1965 as the *Scalpay* (I).

Operating across Loch Leven in 1966, then, were the *Glen Mallie*, *Glen Duror* and *Glen Loy*, as well as the smaller passenger launches. This proved to be the final year of the passenger crossings and even with lights now fitted at the slipways, the passenger service ceased at dusk. By now the *Glen Duror* was only five years old but her wooden deck was deteriorating badly. To remedy this she was re-decked and the other

Right: The **Glen Mallie** entered service in 1959 when this photograph was taken. One man swings her turntable and six cars with ease while the vessel sits in the shallowest of water. *(GL Watson Ltd 2012)*

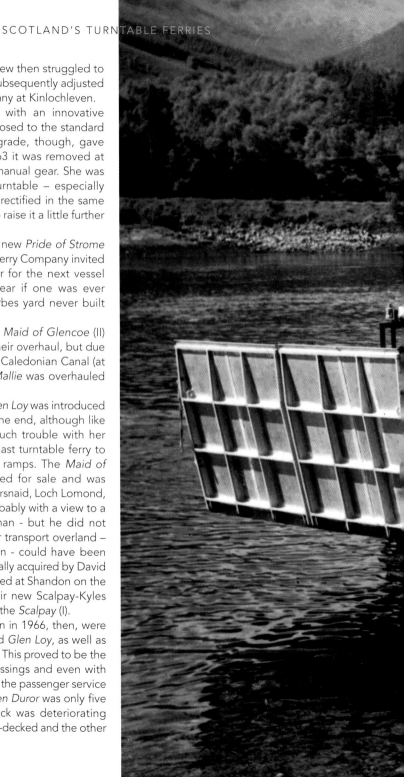

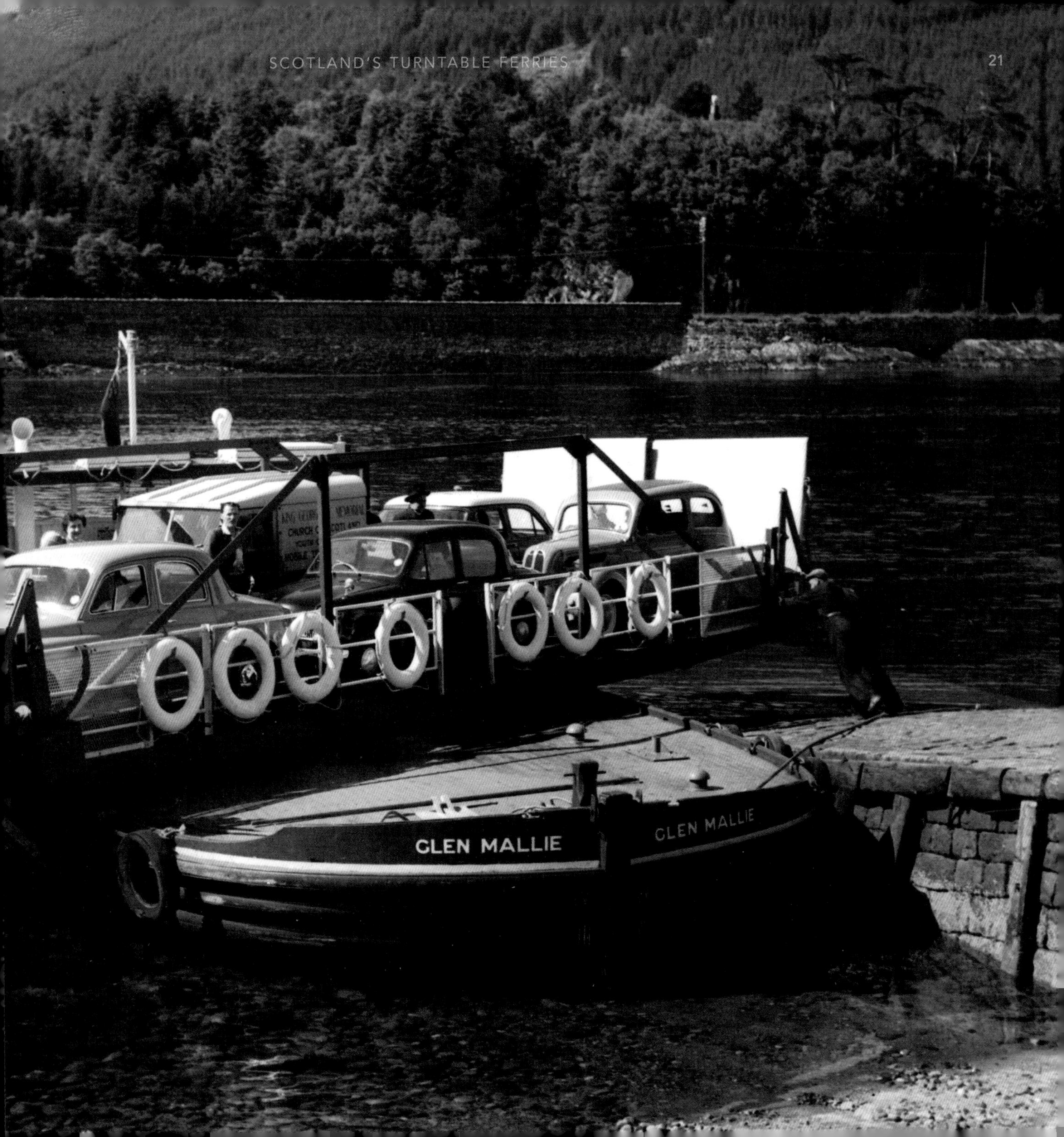
GLEN MALLIE
GLEN MALLIE

Below: The *Glenachulish* approaches North Ballachulish as work on the bridge continues unabated. *(John Newth)*

two vessels had more deck ventilators fitted to reduce the risk of rot. To save crew-time – and, perhaps, with some cynicism as to their honesty – the Company was by now employing shore-staff to collect fares from vehicles before they boarded. In a sensible (if only tacitly acknowledged) compromise, Edward Barrow recalls, these women began an hour or so after the first sailings of the day and knocked off an hour or so before the end and the crew were allowed to collect and keep fares in these hours for themselves; 'the skim', as it was called, seems a reasonable perk.

These were lightly built ferries and never intended to have a long lifespan – a wooden-built Ballachulish boat was old by fifteen, and the *Glen Mallie*'s long service was latterly, be it remembered, in summer-only duty. But they were attractive craft with some ingenious design touches: the turntable was locked not only into seagoing position with four bolts – and six, if for a long voyage to overhaul – but could additionally be locked at two different angles across the ship; at forty-five or ninety degrees. (In fact they were usually moored in this position, with the vehicle-deck thrown straight across the boat, when

the ramps acted as paravanes and kept the boat bow to the wind.)

The final vessel to be constructed for use at Ballachulish is, today, the last turntable ferry still operating. She was ordered in August 1968 and was built as an apprentices' project at the Ailsa Shipbuilding Company in Troon. The yard had also constructed the last (and substantial) turntable ferries for Kyleakin, and the lads built this Ballachulish ship with unusually thick steel plates which perhaps goes some way to explaining survival well into her fifth decade.

Named the *Glenachulish*, she entered service in April 1969. She was the first (and only) steel vessel constructed for use at Ballachulish and the last steel turntable ferry ever built. Her arrival allowed the *Glen Mallie* to be sold to Glenelg. Murdo MacKenzie paid £2,000 for her; years later, she would once again be dethroned by the Ailsa-built ferry.

The *Glenachulish* and the *Glen Loy* were now the principal vessels, with the *Glen Duror* in reserve. Her crew seem to have been particular characters, recalls Ewen Kennedy Henderson of Strontian, who had not even been born when the service ceased. 'What a

Left: This 1973 view of the *Glen Loy* shows her leaving South Ballachulish with the northern slipway visible above her bow ramp. *(John Hendy)*

Below: The *Appin Chief* of 1955 also ended her days on the Kylerhea to Glenelg crossing.

squad for *deoch* seemingly... one Hogmanay, they were reported for drinking and the police were waiting at either slipway; my father was a car passenger. They went round in circles in the middle of the narrows until the police went. My father joined in the dramming (actually on his way to pipe in Lochailort House for New Year) and had the pipes with him... They all took turns at the wheel going round in circles. Pipes going, drams, songs - the police got bored and left and they went ashore to the Loch Leven Hotel and enjoyed the bells there and, bleutered, managed to moor the ferry and row ashore. That's good seamanship...'

Edward Barrow recalls mischievously that, if a crewman was quick – there were three per vessel and they would take turns – one could nip into the public bar of the Loch Leven Hotel, by the northern slip, and drain a half-pint and return as his fellows completed loading. On one occasion, though, one jumped the gun, and happily dashed for his ale on tying up – quite forgetting first to unlock and pivot the turntable, lower the ramps, and unload the latest complement of cars. It seems passengers and drivers, trapped aboard (to say nothing of those waiting who wanted to cross) finally made quite a fuss; certainly, the one of the men was disciplined – though not

dismissed – by the Company.

Usually overhauls occurred at the Thornbush Slipway and Engineering Company Ltd near Inverness. With the good service received from Ailsa's yard at Troon, though, it was decided to use the yard for some future overhauls. In practice, Company minutes suggest, only the *Glenachulish* could go to Troon as both the *Glen Duror* and *Glen Loy* were too broad to fit through the Crinan Canal. (This is dubious: in May 1978, the second *Scalpay*, no less beamy, negotiated the canal without difficulty; and the Ailsa-built Kyleakin ferries may have been delivered by it.)

In 1975, as the new Ballachulish bridge fast took shape, Cameron of Lochiel, in his councillor's hat, suggested hopefully that the new Western Isles Islands Council would purchase all three Ballachulish ferries for use at Scalpay and also new services to Eriskay, Berneray or Vatersay. Although Caledonian MacBrayne

already operated to Scalpay they were determined to convert it to a bow-loading operation which involved £80,000 of slipway reconstruction, threatening to withdraw if the work was not completed. The purchase of the three former Ballachulish ferries would therefore be a cheaper option but in the event the Comhairle were not tempted: the two older ferries, after all, were almost life expired while all three were very lightly built for such an exposed environment as the Outer Hebrides, and tidal conditions precluded the use of side-loading craft at Berneray or Eriskay. Had they appreciated the greater inconvenience of bow-loading for Scalpay drivers, they might have chosen otherwise.

Scalpay though, would have a ferry for years to come; after a long campaign, a Ballachulish bridge was approved in 1973 and works had begun on the site by the spring of 1974. The end was nigh.

'I stayed in the Ballachulish Hotel in the last days before the bridge was opened,' John Prebble – whose account of the Massacre of Glen Coe remains definitive – remembered, seventeen years later. 'We were filming in Glen Etive; the final location sequences for 'John Macnab.' Every evening in the residents' lounge the director played traditional jazz, and the assistant floor-manager danced in bare feet. The public bar was full, a noisy wake for the dying car-ferry, and the centre of it was an aged boatmaster in peaked cap and reefer jacket. He had spent a lifetime on Caolas Mhic Phadraig, backward and forward, to and fro in all weathers, countless voyages of five minutes duration. But, as the hour became later, noisier and more maudlin, it was easy to believe, with help from The Glenlivet, that a great deep-water sailor had come home from the sea...'

After a number of delays due to a 'structural fault' – a bolt had snapped, with a spectacular bang, delaying completion by weeks - the new Ballachulish bridge was finally opened, by HM Queen Elizabeth the Queen Mother on 23rd December 1975. The original date of opening had been 4th October, and by then the Ballachulish Ferry Company had sold their vessels; on it they sternly withdrew their service and

began the process of liquidation. Fortunately the Highland Regional Council had bought the most recent boat, the steel-hulled *Glenachulish*, for £15,000 for relief and back-up on their own crossings. The *Glenachulish*, with a Corran crew and without interruption, was able to maintain a Ballachulish service until the bridge eventually opened. She then lay briefly at Corran before finding a final berth (for most of the year, and years thereafter) at the Muirtown Basin in Inverness as back-up on the Kessock service. For a few days in November 1979 emergency, indeed, she had to maintain it single-handed; and she besides relieved regularly at Kylesku, and less frequently at Corran. After the opening of the Kessock Bridge, in July 1982, she was sold to Murdo MacKenzie for his service at Kylerhea.

In 2003 – as part of a back-up strategy should the landslip-prone A890 Strome bypass road be closed for a protracted period – she made successful trial at the old slips on the Loch Carron narrows and when, nine years later, that did indeed happen, the 43-year old veteran maintained a lifeline service over the Strome straits, and with notable success, from 16th January to 22nd March 2012.

The two remaining Ballachulish vessels were also sold. The *Glen Loy* was acquired by UEG Trials of Inverlochy, Fort William for £4,500, for use as a platform at their diver-training school but by the late summer of 1977 the vessel had been stripped to a pontoon, and was no longer on the Mercantile Register. She was photographed beached at Trislaig opposite Fort William by G E Langmuir that July. Her final fate is unknown although a little enclosure for fishing-creels by Trislaig beach – made of her discarded white deck-railings – could still be seen in 1992.

The reserve Ballachulish ferry *Glen Duror* was sold to 'a local man' for £3,000 and was later used in connection with major reconstruction works on the Caledonian Canal at Muirtown and Laggan during 1976–77. She was then beached on the western shore of Loch Lochy a few hundred yards north of Gairlochy, where her hulk remains.

The Ballachulish Ferry Company Ltd was formally wound up on 5th November 1975.

Below: Abandoned on the shores of Loch Lochy are the battered remains of the **Glen Duror**. *(Fred Riley)*

Inset: The abandoned hulk of the **Mamore** at Lochinver. *(Max Pittman)*

The route's second turntable ferry was the *Dhuirnish* of 1956 which was eventually converted to bow loading for the Bute Ferry Company across the Kyles of Bute. A further sale in 1971 saw her very briefly used on a new service linking Port Bannatyne (where she is pictured) and Ardyne Point. (*AM Young*)

BONAWE – Loch Etive (Taynuilt to Bonawe on B845)

The 370-yard Bonawe Ferry crossing had operated since well before the sixteenth century, originally running as a passenger-only service. The ferry worked across Loch Etive only 8 miles from the Connel ferry. The crossing became more important after 1753 when the Lorne Furnace Iron Works was established at Bonawe and a few decades later, the Bonawe Quarry set up on the other side of the loch. All this brought more traffic for the route and the company set about improving the roads in the immediate area. This all helped to establish the route as the premier way across Loch Etive and by the nineteenth century two boats and two ferrymen worked from Bonawe.

Another small passenger ferry crossed the River Awe from Inverawe to the Bonawe ferry slip on the Taynuilt side. This ferry was known as the Penny Ferry and was on an ancient droving route. Travellers and their livestock would then continue across to Bonawe and through the glen to the Shian ferry.

Famous traveller Dorothy Wordsworth crossed at Bonawe in 1803. She thought the ferryman was particularly skilled as the

"lad managed his oars, glorying in the appearance of danger."

A hundred years later in 1903 the railway from Oban to Ballachulish bridged Loch Etive at Connel and the first vehicles were carried across Loch Etive by train in 1909. They were transported on a special working which ran between Connel Ferry station, North Connel station and Benderloch station as long as vehicles were "without petrol and storage batteries", but passengers still had to use the ferry far below the viaduct.

The arrangement at Connel offered little competition to the operations at Bonawe and a rowing boat capable of carrying up to three tons was in operation on the latter route between 1905 and 1914. In 1914 another rowing boat capable of carrying 10 tons entered service, probably in response to changes back down the loch at Connel where the London Midland &

Scottish Railway had opened the rough track alongside the railway for the use of vehicles and pedestrians at periods when no train was in the vicinity. A toll was charged for the privilege of using the bridge.

Back at Bonawe J & A Gardner, who operated the local quarry, planned to upgrade the service to carry vehicles. An order was placed with Hugh MacLean & Sons Ltd of Renfrew to have a vessel ready before 30th March 1937.

The *Deirdre* was named after the heroine in Irish mythology who founded Glen Etive after fleeing Ulster with her lover Naoise. The

Deirdre carried up to four small cars, or one bus or a ten-ton lorry and was the first motorised vessel on the route. Following her commission, the railway company halved their tolls for the Connel Bridge crossing.

In the early days the ferry was in continuous operation between 07.30 and 22.30 and carried the mail to Bonawe. During the Second World War she did not operate and was in fact sent to Orkney to assist with the building of the Churchill Barriers which formed Scapa Flow's submarine defences. In her absence the crossing was operated by small boats. The *Deirdre* returned to Bonawe after the war but did not re-enter service, being beached in the West Harbour at Bonawe until eventually destroyed by burning – suggesting that she was riddled with rot or shipworm.

The small boats which had operated the crossing during the war continued to provide a passenger-only service but it is not known whether a boat large enough to handle a vehicle was kept ready. Quarry vehicles would have had to travel along Loch Etive and over the Connel Bridge before turning south-east at Barcaldine before reaching the quarry. It is recalled that the narrowness of the track way - laid beside the rails - damaged the tyre walls of the lorries and this was probably one of many factors which led the quarry company, J & A Gardner, to place a new vessel on the route in 1956.

Named *Dhuirnish*, she was built by Noble's yard in Fraserburgh and was the last vehicle ferry on the crossing. She could carry up to four cars, depending on size, along with up to 12 passengers and was supplied with twin Gleniffer engines which gave an

operating speed of 7.5 Knots. The *Dhuirnish* was much larger than the *Deirdre* and as a result, in 1957 the piers at both Bonawe and Taynuilt were heightened to accommodate her.

She suffered only one major mishap during her service at Bonawe, when in the mid 1960s she sank but was raised shortly afterwards by one of Gardner's cargo boats, the *St Kentigern*.

In 1966, the last year of the Bonawe crossing, the charge was 5 shillings (25p) for a car and 3d for a foot passenger. The rival bridge at Connel was more expensive, at 6 shillings (30p) for a car, with a width limit on the bridge of 6ft 6 inches. The *Dhuirnish* ran between 08.00 and 16.45 Monday to Friday and between 08.00 and 12.00 on Saturdays. There was no Sunday service. It was noted in the AA road book for Scotland for that year that cars were carried only if convenient; the ferry was primarily for quarry traffic.

Late in 1966, as the Connel bridge was adapted to exclusive service by road traffic – the Ballachulish line had closed at Easter – the car ferry service ceased. The *Dhuirnish* was sold to the Bute Ferry Co. Ltd for operation at Colintraive and the remaining passenger service at Bonawe in turn closed on 30th September

The **Deirdre** of 1937 briefly served the route until the start of the war when she was sent to Scapa Flow to assist in the construction of the Churchill Barriers.

Below: The *Dhuirnish* as she appeared at Bonawe from 1956 until 1966 after which she was sold to the Bute Ferry Co.

1967. Also closed were the minor passenger operations still ongoing at Connel, to allow completion of works up on the bridge. Even so, to this day the bridge is still too narrow to allow two-lane operation and traffic lights are in place to control flow.

Although never again to operate with a turntable, the subsequent career of the *Dhuirnish* is worth noting. She was converted to bow-loading and with her capacity accordingly increased to six average-sized cars, was ready to enter service on the Kyles of Bute narrows by late April 1967. She operated alongside the drive through *Eilean Buidhe*, made from plywood, and the bow-loading *Eilean Dhu*. On 13th January 1968, she sank in a gale. She was subsequently raised on 4th February and returned to service soon after repairs at Port Bannatyne. Her return was timely as the *Eilean Dhu* had to be temporarily withdrawn due to ramp damage.

In March 1968 Western Ferries' *Sound of Gigha* was tested on the route, prior to taking up service between Port Askaig on Islay and Feolin on Jura in the following March.

A year later, on Tuesday 18th March 1969 while the *Dhuirnish* was at James Adam & Sons (Ship repairers) Ltd in Gourock having her engines inspected, both the *Eilean Buidhe* and *Eilean Dhu* were damaged in another storm. As a result no vehicle ferry operated at

Colintraive until the *Eilean Buidhe* was patched up to run on one engine from 24th March. The *Dhuirnish* was rushed back, with engines refurbished by the Bergius-Kelvin company on 3rd April. Her return allowed the *Eilean Buidhe* to undergo a thorough overhaul and the *Eilean Dhu* to be raised by the naval boom defence vessel *Kingarth*.

April 1969 saw Scottish Office approval in principle for a bridge to be built over the Kyles of Bute to which the Bute Ferry Co responded by stating they had plans to start a 24-hour service once lighting had been installed at the slipways. They also had ambitions to commission an 11-vehicle ferry for the route.

Neither plan was forthcoming; in fact, the Scottish Office gambit was but a cynical tactic. In December 1969 the Bute Ferry Company was purchased by the Caledonian Steam Packet Company Ltd with the *Eilean Buidhe*, *Eilean Dhu* and *Dhuirnish* also included in the sale. (The CSP and David MacBrayne Ltd were now wholly owned by the Scottish Transport Group – itself owned by the State and accountable to the Scottish Office.)

The new owners used the *Dhuirnish* as the main vessel on the run and in 1970 she was duly joined by the *Portree* (II) from Kyle of Lochalsh iwhich was converted to bow-loading operations at a cost of £20,000. The *Dhuirnish* remained as the secondary

vessel until the *Broadford* (II) appeared (also from Kyle) in June 1971 and was also converted to bow loading.

The *Dhuirnish* was then offered for sale and was purchased two months later by local scrap-merchant Robert Beattie of Rothesay for just £900. He intended to use her on a new service linking Port Bannatyne with the mainland at Ardyne Point in direct competition with the operations at Colintraive. A war of words with the Caledonian Steam Packet ensued as the company tried to hold him to the customary term in their bill of sale: that the vessel could not be used in competition with any of their services. Mr Beattie claimed he did not sign such an agreement and much to the CSP's dismay, the vessel introduced the rival crossing. It was brief. Her skipper was familiar with the vessel as he had worked for the Bute Ferry Company, and on her first day in service, Saturday 21st August, she flew the skull and crossbones on the 18 minute crossing which she operated for free! On the following day she operated as normal, with the charge for a vehicle and passengers being 50p whilst pedestrians travelled for free. The following weekend she was unfortunately stranded by the tide on the slipway at Port Bannatyne. Robert Beattie's grand visions, if the Ardyne ferry became a success, had included a service from Rothesay to Largs using a landing craft with capacity for 50 vehicles. Nothing ever came of the Largs project; his Ardyne-Port Bannatyne ferry only lasted a fortnight.

In mid-September 1971 the laird of Little Cumbrae, Mr Peter Kay – who was also Chairman of Highland Engineering Ltd - acquired the vessel and she was later noted at Oban as a barge/ tender on Kerrera before being sold to the farm at Midpark Farm Beach at Inchmarnock. The *Dhuirnish* was pictured alongside the Caledonian MacBrayne 'Island' class vessel *Bruernish* in October 1985, unloading a trailer on the island, but is thought to have been abandoned soon after.

The **Dhuirnish** was converted to a bow loader and is seen serving on the Kyles of Bute crossing between Rhubodach and Colintraive.

This 1967 view of the **Ben Keil** discharging cars also illustrates her split wheel-house linked by a small passenger cabin.
(Iain Thornber)

CORRAN - Loch Linnhe (Nether Lochaber to Ardgour)

The Loch Linnhe narrows mark an ancient drovers' route linking mainland Lochaber with the Morvern and Ardnamurchan peninsulas to the west. The crossing – saving travellers an involved 40-mile journey round Loch Linnhe and Loch Eil – takes its name from the scythe-like point on the Ardgour side where stands today's lighthouse: 'corran' is Gaelic for 'sickle.' With a turbulent tide-race and high mountains funnelling the fierce Highland winds, this is a much less sheltered passage than Ballachulish and one of the most exposed crossings on which turntable ferries served. The historic (and slightly less vulnerable) passage, though, was half a mile to the north of the car ferry service finally established some seventy-five years ago: another instance of the blessings of motor-power.

In his splendid history of the district, 'Romantic Lochaber', Donald B MacCulloch noted the poignant fear of an old woman, long ago, cleared with her people from a local hamlet to the Americas. Did she not dread the long voyage across the Atlantic, someone asked? 'Och, no,' she said, 'if we get through the Corran narrows, we have nothing to fear...' Ironically, one of the nastiest of Highland lairds – and responsible for many such evictions – met a

sticky end here: in 1828 Alasdair Ranaldson MacDonnell of Glengarry, a vain parakeet of a man, was aboard Henry Bell's paddle steamer *Stirling* when, amidst a fierce storm, she grounded at Inverscaddle Bay, Ardgour. Only one man drowned - a butler to another Chief, Macdonald of Clanranald – but MacDonnell, leaping for his life, slipped on the rocks and fatally broke his head. The skerry is still known locally as *Sgeir mhic 'ic Alasdair* – 'Glengarry's Rock.'

We have a still older, no less robust tale of the ferry from the fifteenth century. At that time the MacMaster clan had charge of it, holding the Ardgour side of the crossing while Donald MacLean was his neighbour to the south and west. MacLean with the support of his father, Lachlan MacLean of Duart on Mull, as well as the help of Skye kin, attacked and defeated the MacMasters, thus acquiring Ardgour. The Chief of the MacMasters fled to the ferry where he expected to be taken across by the ferryman, a fellow clansman. The ferryman declined to convey the chief and, in the curious honour-code of the Highlands, Donald MacLean ordered that the sailor be "strung from his own oars until dead" for his betrayal.

Corran played its part in the 1745 uprising, for supplies from the generally detested Government garrison at Fort William were shipped up Loch Linnhe

from Oban. As the boats passed through the narrows, the locals shot at them and, in reprisal, the homesteads of Ardgour were later burned to the ground.

Originally the ferryboats voyaged between mere shingle beaches, but in 1817 piers were built at either side to aid loading and unloading.

The MacLean family held the route until the 1930s when they handed it over to the Argyll County Council. The council in turn advertised a lease for the crossing in 1934 and the successful bidders were James Mackintosh and Donald Buchanan. The Mackintosh's would be linked to the ferry for nearly half a century; in 1940 Mr Buchanan retired and the ferry was left in the sole charge of the family.

Anne Mackintosh has recorded her memories of these leisurely early days before a vehicular service –

Well, when I remember Corran Ferry first, I was a very small child, and in those days the ferry was run by a man by the name of Donald Buchanan - originally it was a rowing boat he had going across - and to call the ferryman there was a bell hanging on an iron post at the ferry here, and a rope on it, and the passengers came along and rang the bell at the ferry and Donald just came across when it suited himself; there was no great hurry at all. Of course, people didn't rush around in those days at all. And eventually he managed to get a motor launch and things were a wee bit easier for him and, of course, the service improved with a motor launch. But with a hotel on both sides Donald was inclined to get lost now and again, and sometimes forget that the boat was tied up at the jetty. And the tide would go out, and, of course, the ferry had to be off until the tide came in and lifted it off the shore again...

Prior to the introduction of vehicle ferries in the 1930s, the actual site of the crossing was moved south of its original location and the run was serviced by passenger motorboats; one named *An Easdale* after where she had served prior to her arrival at Corran. In the 1920s it seems – for a photograph survives - the Ballachulish ferry *Glencoe* (I) made a special run to offload an ambulance on the Ardgour slipway. There may have been other such runs for vehicles but the need for a dedicated Corran car ferry was evident.

The route's first turntable ferry was a 20-year old former lifeboat which was purchased in 1934 by

Buchanan and Mackintosh. The winter of 1934 was spent converting her to carry cars and the 'Western Times' reported in January 1935 that it was hoped to have a service for vehicles in operation by Easter.

She duly began service in April, although seems to have been a nameless craft. In the event, her career was brief. At Ballachulish, the *Glencoe* (I) was redundant on the arrival of the larger *Maid of Glencoe* (I) and was swiftly purchased for Corran duty. The former lifeboat disappears from the record and the *Glencoe* (I) appears to have operated from Ardgour

Left: Known at Corran as simply the 'Tough', the vessel was originally the *Glencoe* (II) at Ballachulish. *(Robert Grieves collection)*

Below: The *Maid of Glengour* loading at Corran. From this image, it can be appreciated that this was one of the most exposed of turntable ferry crossings. *(Macintosh family collection)*

Above: The **Garven** is unusually seen moored in the Caledonian Canal on her way to refit at Inverness.
(Macintosh family collection)

Below: The **Garven** approaches Ardgour.
(Macintosh family collection)

without a formal name being locally remembered only as 'the White Boat'.

Unfortunately she was plagued with mechanical problems and was frequently – and lengthily - out of service. Even so, by May 1936, 239 cars and trucks had been borne over the narrows and another turntable ferry was hastily chartered (and in time bought outright) to ensure reliable service for that summer. This was the younger Ballachulish boat *Glencoe* (II), displaced by the new *Queen of Glen Albyn*. At Corran she was first known merely 'the Grey Boat' and later honoured with the nickname of 'Tough'. She was certainly of heavier construction than her predecessor and better suited to the rather crude slipways in use on the crossing.

As the 'Tough' assumed Corran service, 'the White Boat' was laid up just south of the piers on the Ardgour side for serious refit. The work was carried out by Archie Henderson of Mallaig, who built a steaming-box for shaping of new timbers and an additional fire, by the old jetty, for heating tar and pitch. Her engines

were also reconditioned by Bergius mechanics.

Unfortunately the day before 'The White Boat' was ready for her re-launch, in mid-December 1936, a south-westerly gale howled up Loch Linnhe and she was blown off the beach. On the morning of Sunday 20th December all that could be seen was her bow sticking out of the water. It was a forlorn fate for our very first turntable ferry; the 'Tough' remained in service alone.

A new ferry was needed and was duly constructed by John Henderson & Sons, boatbuilders in Mallaig. Delivered in 1937, the timber craft was thirty-six feet long and with a 16-feet beam. She drew about three and a half feet and cost £650. Although rather larger than the 'Tough' she could carry but a single car as the turntable of the older vessel was recycled when building her. Originally un-named, she was referred to as the 'Mallaig Boat' but later gained the name *North Argyll*. As the 'Tough's turntable was used on the *North Argyll*, it seems that the older boat was discarded.

The *North Argyll* was not as strong as the previous vessels and had later to be reinforced with uprights between keel and deck-beams. Her deck also leaked due the planking being laid 'tongue in groove' style as opposed to the usual caulking with pitch.

In September 1938, Donald Buchanan was fined £4 for exceeding his passenger limit by carrying 17 fare-paying passengers when the craft was certificated for only twelve. In the same month the *North Argyll* broke down on passage. She had a car on board as well as a few passengers and ended up drifting over a mile. She was duly rescued by the yacht *Orpheus*, and towed back to Ardgour.

In 1939 the lessee of the ferry proposed to have another vehicle ferry built but this time to make it 5 feet longer than the *North Argyll*. With the national emergency, this vessel never appeared but the proposal makes plain that traffic on the crossing was increasing.

Due to a number of small mishaps during the early 1940s, minor changes were made to the *North Argyll*. It was deemed appropriate to place blocks under the wheels of each car using the ferry while skids were placed along the sides of the turntable itself.

The *North Argyll* operated throughout the Second World War, although ill-maintained (twin brothers from the Hebrides were in desultory charge) and ever more

prone to protracted breakdown. A petition was raised by cross residents of the Ardnamurchan peninsula in 1941, complaining that a vehicle ferry had not been in service for a while. In the spring of 1942 she was out of service for a whole month in March and April and only passengers were conveyed. At least twice during the war the *North Argyll* sank dolefully at her moorings – which makes such absences understandable – and, by the end of Hitler's war, her engines were in desperate need of replacement. The unimpressive twins, whose attention to maintenance was minimal, quit their duties in 1945.

The 1940s saw major improvements in the road network around Ardnamurchan and Moidart and over £500,000 was spent on upgrading the road surfaces and the slipways at Nether Lochaber and Ardgour. The work on the slips was carried out with a 75% grant from the Road Fund.

With better roads and yet more vehicles, a new, larger ferry was increasingly essential. In 1944, Henderson's of Mallaig offered speculatively to build one for £1,560 but this was declined. An order was then placed with James Noble of Fraserburgh for a 2-car craft in 1945, but unfortunately, during post war years the waiting time for a new engine was up to two years. It was a time of desperate expediencies. A local farmer had purchased 'The White Boat's' old 2-cylinder engine which was now retrieved and hastily installed in the *North Argyll*, allowing the 4-cylinder engine to be overhauled at a local garage. After refurbishment, the 4-cylinder engine was taken to Fraserburgh to be put into the new boat.

The *Maid of Glengour* was launched in 1946 and could carry two cars or one lorry. She did not sail to Corran under her own power, however, but was towed by a fishing boat through the Caledonian Canal. Once she arrived it took a day and a half of work to get the engine running after which the old *North Argyll* was abandoned on the beach.

Inevitably there were teething troubles. The new ship was not long in operation when a crankshaft broke, quite disabling her. A Bergius engineer soon ascertained that the local garage had not reassembled the engine correctly after its reconditioning. All was put right and the *Maid of Glengoul* quickly settled down soon proving to be a much more reliable boat than the *North Argyll* and, in addition, she was totally watertight. She operated well, apart from when going astern, but this was easily managed with some experience.

Until May 1947, the busiest day ever seen on the Corran crossing had brought twenty-two vehicles seeking passage. Later that year, during the Scottish six-day motorcycle trials, sixty-nine vehicles were conveyed in a single day. Only a year after the new boat's arrival, yet more tonnage was needed.

James Noble of Fraserburgh again tendered, and a new, substantial ferry was delivered in June 1949. Named the *Garven* she could carry four small cars. Her hull design was far superior to that of the *Maid of Glengour* and, with a Gardner diesel engine she handled well. As built she had no wheelhouse – crew comfort was still not a Highland priority – but in later life the *Garven* acquired one during her annual Inverness overhaul. One drawback was her salt-water cooling system which caused bad 'scaling' in the engine. This was later rectified by employing a closed fresh water system which had a heat exchanger outside the hull. Once the *Garven* had settled in, the

Below: This June 1971 view of the Corran Narrows shows the ***Ben Keil*** alongside on the left as the ***Gleann Mhor*** approaches. *(David Parsons)*

Above: The **Gleann Mhor** in the Caledonian Canal during August 1984.

Below left: The mighty 9-car **Lochaber** was the route's final turntable ferry and the last such vessel ever built. *(Brian Maxted)*

Below right: The **Ben Keil** entered service in 1959 and was replaced by the **Lochaber** in 1973.

Maid of Glengour was sold locally.

In 1949 the 'Blue' guide to Scotland states opaquely that a one-car ferry was in operation; in fact, the *Maid of Glengour* could actually carry two cars. One assumes that the still larger *Garven* was delivered after the guide's researchers had carried out their checks.

The Mackintosh family still had charge of the Corran service and brothers Peter and Alistair crewed under a doughty skipper, Peter MacQueen. The timetable for 1950 was shows us that the vehicle ferry operated continuously between 08.00 and 20.00 between May and September. During the remaining months it started at 08.30; a passenger launch ran until 21.15 all year round. In 1953 the service ran from 08.00 until 19.45 on weekdays and on Sundays between 10.30 and 19.45. In winter the service finished at dusk. The charge for a car with a driver and passenger was 6 shillings (30p).

A new, 6-car twin-screw ferry was forthcoming in 1959, when the *Ben Keil* was delivered from Noble's yard. She boasted both elevated, enclosed steering-positions and – for the first time – a covered shelter, below and between them, for foot-passengers. The *Garven* was retained meanwhile for back-up and relief. The *Ben Keil* in turn was followed in 1964 by the *Gleann Mhor*, a still more impressive Noble built craft.

She was beamier – able to squeeze on nine small cars – and boasted spring-braced ramps rather than the usual counterweight design. Both these ferries were certificated to carry large numbers of passengers if required (60 and 80 respectively); and they also brought a new livery: hitherto, the Corran ferries had been one monotonous grey but now vehicle-deck, rails and ramps became a cheery red. The *Garven*, now redundant, was sold to Wiggins Teape Ltd for deployment at Corpach Basin, their rising pulp-mill and its jetties. The ambitious plant duly opened in April 1966.

The Corran ferry was a key link in the MacBrayne bus network and local service buses from Fort William to Strontian, as well as day and half day excursions to Ardnamurchan and Loch Shiel used the ferry. The operators of the ferry in the 1960s charged 10 shillings (50p) for a bus to cross and 4d for each passenger on board. Completion of a new road from Lochailort to Acharacle, in 1967, ended MacBrayne's passenger service on Loch Sheil and further increased Corran traffic.

With the new, bigger boats the Nether Lochaber slip proved inadequate at low tides, and was now rebuilt. Floodlighting was installed in 1966 at a cost of £400 to enable the ferry to be used after dark if an

emergency required it. Since 1973, the opening of CalMac's back door service to Mull via Lochaline and Fishnish has also assisted in the route's popularity and at that time, the service was operated on lease by Alex & Mary Mackintosh. In 1975 the Highland Regional Council took direct control over the operation.

The ferry was running smoothly with the two large ferries but one frustrating point was the weight limit imposed which meant that most heavy goods vehicles had to drive around the top of Loch Eil. Also the increase in vehicles carried was far more than expected. In 1971 65,256 vehicles were carried between April and September. The following year 72,460 were carried in the same period: an increase of 7,204 vehicles during the twelve-months.

It was realised that a larger vessel was needed and the route's final turntable ferry was the *Lochaber*, which replaced the *Ben Keil* late in 1973. The *Ben Keil* was noted at Crinan in the late 1970s although her final fate is as yet unknown.

The mighty, 64-feet long *Lochaber* was also built by James Noble at Fraserburgh and could carry as many as 100 passengers if required. Her build was financed with the help of a loan of £30,000 from the North West Securities Group which was to be paid back over a period of seven years. The last turntable ferry ever built, she was besides the very largest in capacity (though exceeded by the latter Kyleakin ferries in length and gross tonnage) and could accommodate nine cars in three rows of three. In her first year of operation, she seemed almost too big: fully laden, her vast turntable proved extremely difficult for her crew

After withdrawal, the *Lochaber* was used in connection with fish farm operations but was driven ashore and wrecked in 1996. *(Iain Thornber)*

to work, and there were long delays. In 1974 hydraulic machinery was installed to ease operation, and the angles of her ramps were adjusted to prevent damage to vehicles when loading and unloading. The following year the Ardgour slip was rebuilt as when the tide was very high, the *Lochaber* struggled to berth and discharge her vehicles.

Considering the exposed nature of the crossing and the early, unprepossessing vessels, it is to the great credit of its operators that no tragedy ever occurred. Anne Mackintosh recalled the most serious incident, in a rather serious storm, was when the laden ferry waded over from Ardgour, found herself quite unable to draw in at the Nether Lochaber slip, and

Below left: The launch of the *Gleann Mhor* at Fraserburgh in 1964. *(courtesy of Steven Munro)*

Below centre: The former Kessock ferry *Rosehaugh* was transferred to Corran in 1982

Below right: Instantly recognisable by her huge turntable 'A' frames, the *Lochaber* prepares to berth at Corran. *(Morag MacKinnon)*

Below: Today's scene at Corran with the huge *Corran* arriving while the reserve vessel *Maid of Glencoul* is on the buoys in the loch. *(John Hendy)*

could not safely return. There was nothing for it but to let the current take her down 'and ride out the gale in the mouth of a river round the point, and she stayed there for two whole days.' All aboard were quickly rescued, but the cars could not be retrieved until the weather had abated.

As tourism had increased remorselessly, one incessant confusion – especially by visitors heading south – constantly amused or vexed the Corran ferry crew: the number of drivers who queued and boarded at Nether Lochaber, convinced they were in fact catching the Ballachulish ferry. Even when a sign was erected – PLEASE NOTE THIS IS NOT BALLACHULISH FERRY – it made bewilderingly little

difference. Chortling visitors would bait deckhands, as they trundled off for the wilds of Ardnamurchan, with the question, 'Why does your sign say this isn't the Ballachulish ferry when it is?' Anne Mackintosh sighed, in interview.

"We sometimes get people crossing here thinking that they're crossing Ballachulish Ferry. They either don't read their maps properly, or they are using an old map which still shows Ballachulish Ferry, knowing that there's a bridge there now. And they may be fifteen, thirty miles away from the ferry on the other side when they suddenly realise that they still haven't reached Glencoe and their intention is to be on the road south. Then they turn up back at the ferry and

they get very annoyed to be charged for coming back again. They think they ought to get back free, although it's been their own mistake going across here.... One man came back one night in a great state, about eleven o'clock, to the ferryman, knocked him up and said would he not get the boat out to take him across? And he was towing a caravan too. He could easily just stop at the roadside and spend the night in his caravan and cross first thing in the morning but he had gone about thirty-five miles before he realised he was on the wrong road...

Another day somebody came along, got onto the boat and asked the ferrymen if that was the Cuillins on the other side and he couldn't be convinced that he wasn't crossing over to Skye. Just because it was a ferry, they all think that they're going over to Skye because I think this is the ferry they hear more about. Oh, I'm sure the ferrymen have plenty of laughs to tell..."

In 1975, Alex and Mary Mackintosh gave up their lease on the service, which passed to the direct control of the new Highland Regional Council. That December saw the opening of the Ballachulish Bridge a few miles away, and the Council's acquisition of the redundant *Glenachulish*, which lay at Corran for a spell and, over the next seven years – despite her low power and light construction – gave very occasional relief. Her primary importance was for back-up at Kessock and from 1976 she was generally stationed at Inverness, as well as relieving annually at Kylesku.

In 1977 the *Scalpay* (II) had been made redundant in the Western Isles by the upgrading of the slipways to allow the *Morvern* to take over at Scalpay. In July 1977 the former Skye ferryboat was retrieved from a remote Scalpay cove, chugged for emergency DTI survey at Stornoway (she had not been overhauled since October 1975) and then sailed south, by Kyle of Lochalsh, on charter to Highland Regional Council at a time when the *Gleann Mhor* was delayed whilst undergoing a major refit at Crinan.

The *Scalpay* (II) duly took up service at Corran on 14th July alongside the *Lochaber*. Unfortunately, she failed to operate a full day in service on the 16th as her turntable bearing seized but was back in service the next day until the *Gleann Mhor* returned in the first week of August. As the *Gleann Mhor* broke down shortly after her return, the *Scalpay* (II) was again used,

until one of her own engines also broke down. She was towed dismally from Corran by the Caledonian MacBrayne 'Small Island Class' ferry *Eigg* on Sunday 7th August, laid up for some months at Lochaline, and never saw passenger service again.

In 1982, after the opening of the Kessock Bridge, the corner-loading *Rosehaugh* was now redundant and in due course was transferred to Corran to become the main vessel on the route, with the *Lochaber* being retained for reserve duties. At a later refit two of the *Rosehaugh*'s four side-ramps were removed. The *Gleann Mhor* was sold in 1983 and ended her days at Ulva working as a barge and her hulk may still remain there.

In June 1985 following the arrival of the 1975 Ardrossan built corner-loader *Maid of Glencoul* from Kylesku – that service too, had been replaced by a new bridge - the *Lochaber* was beached at Ardgour and advertised for sale. She was purchased by Marine Harvest Ltd for their fish farm operations on Loch Sunart and subsequently re-engined. In 1996, the former Corran ferry was driven ashore and wrecked after breaking her moorings in a storm. The wreck was demolished several years later and the remains buried in a landfill site near Strontian. A talented young

Below: Built in 1937 and simply known as 'the Mallaig Boat', the **North Argyll** served at Corran but was not a particularly successful addition to the service. *(Macintosh family collection)*

musician, Ewen Kennedy Henderson – whose father was her last skipper – has a set of bagpipes made from several of her oak timbers.

The *Maid of Glencoul* operated as the main ferry at Corran, with the *Rosehaugh* as reserve, until 2001 when the present incumbent, the *Corran*, was introduced. She is an impressive 150-passenger, 30 car ferry with a fixed vehicle deck and side ramps, built at Hull for £2.9 million. Her arrival allowed the *Rosehaugh* to be sold to MacDonald Ferries, operating from Invergordon supplying oil rigs. The *Maid of Glencoul* remains as the back-up vessel on the last ferry crossing still operated by Highland Council (the successor to the Highland Regional Council). For some weeks late in 2010 she maintained the service solo when the Nether Lochaber slip required urgent repair and, after an outcry deterred the Council from closing the crossing completely in

the interim, only the smaller vessel could use a temporary floating jetty nearby. Until a bridge spans the Corran narrows – and that remains an unlikely prospect – the ferry reigns supreme.

Above right: The **Gleann Mhor** approaches Nether Lochaber.

Right: A wonderful picture of a spotless **Lochaber** on her sea trials off Fraserburgh in 1974. *(courtesy of Steven Munro)*

CUAN – Isle of Luing to Isle of Seil – (on B8003).

The 500 yards which separate Luing and Seil, south of Oban, are today the preserve of the 40-passenger, six-car corner-loading ferry *Belnahua* which is currently operated by Argyll & Bute Council.

There has been a ferry here for hundreds of years and traditionally this was a point, where at slack water, the famous Luing cattle would be swum across to Seil for the drove roads to Falkirk and Crieff. Early records of the link's history are scarce but we have a report from September 1888 - when the Cuan ferryman, John MacIntyre rescued Dr Gordon from his capsized boat *Gipsy*. In 1899 lights were installed at the ferry berths and in October the ferry toiled to bear six hundred sheep across while sixty cattle swam the sound.

With the advent of the steamship, Luing became a regular port of call from Glasgow with cargo-boats and puffers bringing all kinds of supplies. They dropped off coal and goods at Toberonochy and Blackmill Bay, diminishing the importance of the Cuan Sound ferry.

A flat-bottomed barge which used six oars was in use during the 1920s and the first car was precariously conveyed in 1923, boarding the craft via planks. In the 1940s an ex-whaling boat was used as a passenger vessel, towing a cattle barge when necessary. The ferry became more significant as motor-transport increased but it was only in 1953 that the turntable ferry *Maid of Luing* - she could carry two large cars, or sixty cattle and 'some passengers' - was introduced.

The new timber vessel was built for Argyll County

An early picture of the *Maid of Luing* with a livestock lorry on her turntable. As can be seen, the three-man crew are struggling to swing their heavier than usual cargo.
(John Hendy collection)

Council by the ubiquitous James Noble (Boatbuilders) Ltd of Fraserburgh. She was the only turntable ferry to have her wheelhouse for'ard and this lent her a distinctive look. Her skipper was a Second World War veteran and Tarbert Loch Fyne fisherman, John MacAllister who remained in command until, and indeed after, her withdrawal. The low power generated by her single 48-hp Gardner engine caused frequent problems during her career and the Board of Trade restricted her operation, not allowing her to operate for three hours at the beginning of each flood tide, nor for two hours at the start of each ebb tide.

In 1956 the *Maid of Luing* ran between 08.00 and 18.00 during the summer (March to September) and between 09.00 and 16.00 during winter (October to February). She gave no Sunday service. A passenger launch operated in the early mornings and the evenings during the week.

Above: Now adorned in Admiralty grey paint, the **Maid of Luing** is seen during 1970. *(David Parsons)*

Right: Busy times on the Cuan ferry as the **Maid of Luing** prepares to embark livestock. *(Brian Maxted collection)*

On Sundays the passenger-launch sailed between 11.00 and 13.00 then between 15.00 and 18.00 (or dusk, whichever was earlier) provided it could be operated by a single man.

Like the Kylesku ferry, this was a council-operated ferry and, like the Kylesku ferry it was free. The time allowed for each crossing was fifteen minutes – most of it, in fact, consumed by loading and unloading, rather than on actual passage. Timetables today indicate a crossing under five minutes, suggesting a much faster turn round.

The new *Belnahua* was built by the Campbeltown Shipyard at a cost of £20,000 in 1972 - the same cost as it was for converting the *Portree* (II) to bow-loading operations at Colintraive two years earlier. The *Maid of Luing* was kept in reserve for three years but in 1975 she was taken to the nearby island of Shuna and abandoned there. Her hull can still be seen on its northern shore.

In 1978 the former Ballachulish ferry *Glen Mallie*, then in service at Glenelg, was chartered for Cuan service during the *Belnahua*'s annual overhaul. Today the 40-year old vessel operates to a relaxed timetable with Sundays off during the winter when a passenger vessel, *Torsa* operates. She is relieved by the local landowner's vessel, *Grey Dog*.

Left: The hulk of the **Maid of Luing** can still be seen abandoned on nearby Shuna.

Below left: During 1978, the Glenelg – Kylerhea ferry **Glen Mallie** was chartered for the annual overhaul period of the **Belnahua**. (Brian Maxted collection)

Below: The Cuan ferry is today maintained by the side loading ferry **Belnahua**.

DORNIE (also known as the Aird ferry) – Loch Duich, Loch Alsh, Loch Long (Ardelve to Totaig & Dornie on A87)

A ferry operated at Dornie, in the parish of Lochalsh, since at least the early eighteenth century. This was an unusual passage by the confluence of three sea-lochs and therefore three slipways were involved. Road-access to Lochalsh from any direction – Skye, Glenshiel or Lochcarron – necessitated a ferry crossing and today we readily forget that, but for the railway to Kyle, it was to all intents and purposes an island.

Ardelve (east of Kyle of Lochalsh) was the base for the ferry service which called at both Dornie and Totaig across Loch Duich. An unnamed and most basic turntable ferry commenced around 1920 and the charge in 1929 to cross with a vehicle between Ardelve and Dornie was 10 shillings (50p). The same charge was levied at Strome; but the Dornie service was maintained even on Sundays and Bank Holidays.

Left: A wonderfully evocative photograph of the first turntable ferry service to be lost when replaced by a bridge in 1940. With the iconic Eilean Donan castle in the background, the un-named turntable ferry prepares to load a small charabanc.

Below: The Aird ferry is shown leaving Dornie in 1938. *(Falkirk Museums)*

Not for the faint hearted - rowing a plank-loaded ferry across the loch in the early years of the twentieth century. (Neil King collection)

The wooden-hulled ferry could accommodate one vehicle on the turntable deck. There was, of course no covered accommodation for passengers or crew. In the 1930s the turntable was rebuilt, and its timber rails replaced with metal. She was at times assisted by a flat-bottomed barge which was rowed across, or towed behind a small motor launch. By 1940 her normal hours of operation were from eight in the morning to ten at night.

Things could be fraught at Dornie, as the Rev'd Kenneth A MacRae, recorded in his diary in September 1928. 'The terrific hills at Keppoch taxed my driving powers, and coming down at Dornie ferry we got a bit of a fright as I could not get my car to halt, so steep was the decline, until we had run right out on the boat-slip...'

Plans for a toll-bridge were approved in 1936 despite a degree of local opposition. Some called for a road around the head of Loch Long via Killilan, or

for a chain-ferry instead but bridge construction began in 1938.

The new, rather elegant but single-track structure was completed in April 1940, though the opening ceremony was delayed from Monday 15th to Thursday 30th of the month. 750 feet in length and 21.5 feet wide, it bore the highway over fifteen concrete spans set forty feet above the water level. The first day was toll free but from 1st May a toll was levied for those wishing to cross. Mr John C Matheson was employed from March 1940 as collector; he had to be available from 07.00 until 23.00 and was paid £3-10s (£3.50) a week. In 1946 the tolls were abolished, the Dornie Bridge being belatedly regarded as an integral part of the national road network.

A car ferry service continued, though, from the Ardelve slip to Totaig until at least 1947 but by 1949 it had become a passenger-only service.

In 1964 Mr Murdo McRae of Dornie resigned as

Ardelve in 1910 as the ferry loads for Dornie. An appropriately dressed chauffeur stands on the side of the ferry guiding operations as the car's proud owner edges it aboard.

ferry operator at Totaig and the County Council's Highways Committee asked Mr Alex Matheson of Druidaig, who held the ferry rights, to operate the ferry himself with an annual subsidy of £200. It is not sure for how long the ferry operated thereafter but it had certainly ceased by 1970.

By the late 1980s the narrow bridge – with traffic lights by then controlling flow of cars – had become a serious bottleneck. A new, broader bridge with a 2-way highway was completed alongside it in 1990, and the older structure demolished. The demise of the Dornie ferry, half a century earlier, had one significant impact: for the first time Kyleakin became much the more convenient route to Skye if travelling from the south, especially given the steep and challenging road to the Glenelg alternative.

Above: This ancient vehicle has been safely stowed and a plank has been laid at right angles behind its rear wheels to prevent slippage. Notice the oars ready to propel the boat across the loch. (Neil King collection)

Left above and below: An SMT (Scottish Motor Traction) coach on the first excursion to the Isle of Skye in 1934. After crossing from Dornie to Ardelve, the intrepid travellers would face a further ferry crossing between Kyle of Lochalsh and Kyleakin.

Below: A passenger launch was also on hand to ferry travellers across Loch Alsh, Loch Duich and Loch Long.

KESSOCK - Beauly Firth & Moray Firth (South Kessock to North Kessock now on the A9)

Although the story of Scotland's turntable ferries is exclusively Highland, all but one were on the western seaboard. The Kessock Ferry was the exception on Scotland's east coast, linking western Inverness across the straits between the Beauly and Moray Firths to the Black Isle.

The service was operated by local families for many generations, the earliest reference dating from 1437. In 1591 the ferry became the property of the Burgh of Inverness but by the seventeenth century the ferry and some land at Kessock was part of the Redcastle Estate. It was this estate that Sir William Fettes purchased in 1825 and in 1841 he placed a steamboat on the run named *Maid of Morven*. He chose, though, to raise fares to pay for the second-hand vessel, jetties and shore shelters, provoking local outcry.

Clyde-built in 1826 by John Wood, the *Maid of Morven* had operated from Glasgow to the West Highlands steaming on alternate weeks to Tobermory and Fort William. In 1835 her sailings had been extended to Cromarty and from there to either Burghead or Invergordon and so she would have been seen regularly passing Kessock.

She assumed the Kessock station after her labours for Robert Napier but the posting was brief. By 1846 she was re-registered at Glasgow and sailing from Fort William while later, it is known that she worked for the Glasgow and Liverpool Steam Shipping Company. The well-travelled steamer was finally broken up in 1850.

In spite of this avowed investment, this Kessock steamboat was soon withdrawn but the fares,

The **Inbhir-Nis** alongside in the Muirtown Basin at Inverness when new in 1953. With higher than usual freeboard and a large passenger cabin, she was very much a 'one off' vessel. The later addition of a raised and split bridge did little to improve her looks. *(Jimmy Nairn & Son collection, Highland Photographic Archive)*

strangely, never fell from their newly increased rate.

By 1876 there were six small sailing ships and rowboats on the run and a steamer was again tried in 1880. Named the *Redcastle,* she lasted less than a year. In 1892 the then Provost of Inverness, Sir Donald MacDonald, undertook the lease of the ferry although the family kept their link with the crossing until the late 1930s.

It would be 1907, though, before Kessock was finally delivered from the age of the coracle when the Kessock Ferry Company installed two small steamers, the *Maud* and *Nellie,* on the service. Both were named after ladies of the Redcastle family and would serve until after the Great War. The concern was dissolved in May 1921, making way for the imaginatively named 'The New Kessock Ferry Company' – formed by Sir Donald's sons. They in turn quickly bought an English pleasure-boat, the *Lowestoft Belle* which had hitherto run short cruises between that port and nearby Great Yarmouth. She could carry a good complement of passengers, and even a few cars, tide and planks and space permitting. On occasion she was joined – or relieved – by the dainty Clyde-built steamer *Ailsa,* a 1906 product of the eponymous shipyard at Troon and which hitherto, apart from excursions from Girvan, had supplied Ailsa Craig (and presumably helped export its curling-stones.) Belonging now to John Watson, she spent most of her time on a service from Invergordon to Inverness via Cromarty, where he lived.

In 1931 the MacDonalds established a separate company with plans to operate a chain-ferry at Kessock, with support and subsidy from Ross and Cromarty County Council. It came to nothing and, in 1935 Kessock Ferry became the sole concern of William Macdonald.

He remained keen to establish a regular vehicle service with a chain-ferry but unfortunately, this was a man with monumental bad luck. He acquired three, in turn, and everyone – in turn – was wrecked on its way to Inverness. The first foundered on Friday 28th February 1936, off the Kintyre coast of Argyll near Campbeltown. Named *Erskine* (III) and dating from 1903, she had served at Erskine for the Clyde Port Authority until displaced by the *Govan Ferry No.3* –

in turn, newly redundant from Renfrew. The boat was, alas, not insured.

Then on Friday 3rd April, MacDonald's second chain-ferry purchase sank in nineteen fathoms of water off St Agnes Head, Cornwall, en route to William MacDonald. She had been one of the King Harry ferries operating across the River Fal between Feock and Philleigh. Finally, in October 1936, a third vessel made its way from the Clyde and up the Firth of Lorne to Banavie to navigate the Caledonian Canal to Inverness. She was another Clyde Port Authority purchase - the former *Renfrew Steam Ferry* (II), built for Renfrew-Yoker service in 1897. After displacement by the *Govan Ferry No.3* at Renfrew in 1903 she had been spare, operating at Erskine for a time before being sold to the hapless Mr Macdonald.

The *Inbhir-Nis* is seen off the South Kessock slipway with her raised bridge.
(John Hendy collection)

Following the opening of the new Kessock Bridge in July 1982, the regular vessel **Rosehaugh** and the turntable ferry **Glenachulish** were laid up for disposal in the Muirtown Basin at Inverness. *(JA Pottinger)*

It was now belatedly discovered, at Banavie, that she was too beamy to fit the locks. The craft was then towed all the way round northern Scotland, via the Pentland Firth, and almost made it before being lost in the outer Moray Firth, off Tarbat Ness, on Thursday 8th April 1937.

The *Lowestoft Belle* was withdrawn in March 1936 and, with no suitable vessel in his possession, Mr MacDonald was obliged to place a rowing boat on the crossing until the *Ailsa* became available in April. He approached the local authorities in December 1936, seeking their assistance; they refused to help and he now threatened to withdraw the service.

The local population thought the answer had come in May 1938 with a magnificent Dutch vessel, renamed the *Black Isle*, equipped to carry twenty cars and even fitted out for livestock. Unfortunately she was found to be too big for the piers and the little motor-boat had to stay.

Again in November 1938 William Macdonald approached the local authority to take over the ferry and, again, they refused; his asking- price of £13,000 was deemed too high. The situation did not improve, and a 'sit-in' was staged aboard that November by sorely tried residents of North Kessock. They demanded the sale of concessionary monthly tickets

– at that time they could only purchase a single for each crossing – and were angry that the last boat of the day never seemed to run at the time advertised. With the ferry unable to operate as the protest continued, the mails were entrusted to a small rowing boat. Unfortunately she was caught in the strong current, the ferry had to dash out to find and rescue her and the demonstration was hastily abandoned.

After yet more complaints of an unsatisfactory service and overcrowding, an investigation was belatedly launched by the Kessock Ferry Joint Committee. It culminated, on 7th June 1938, with seven criminal charges against William James Macdonald:

1. Not maintaining a signal at each side of the ferry for the convenience of passengers.

2. Failure to keep a man at North Kessock pier to aid passengers with the loading and unloading of cargoes.

3. Failure to provide a weighing machine at the North side of the ferry and to keep the piers in proper repair.

4. He did not construct and maintain moveable platforms with rails on both sides of the ferry for the purpose of safely transporting cattle and horses.

5. He failed to construct boards on both sides of the ferry with a table of fares on show.

6. Failure to provide a mechanically propelled boat suitable for traffic of all kinds.

7. He did not provide a service where the last boat of the day from North Kessock was at 8 pm in summer or 7 pm in winter.

All of the above were breaches in the rules and regulations set out by Ross and Cromarty County Council for the running of the ferry. Some twenty-three members of the public gave statements and one even declared that, sometimes, in order to board the boat at certain states of the tide, passengers had to sit on the pier and jump 3 to 4 feet.

The hearing was at Dingwall on 29th December 1938 and took over eight hours. Convicted on all counts, Macdonald was fined £10 – with the alternative of a 30-day prison sentence.

One solution was a Council takeover as under the Harbours, Piers and Ferries (Scotland) act of 1937 the local authority had the power to acquire ferry rights,

by agreement or not. In April 1939, it was duly recommended that the ferry became the joint concern of the Inverness Town Council and the Ross & Cromarty County Council, and, presumably unopposed by William MacDonald, this was duly accomplished in June.

After some dredging work at the piers, the local authorities searched frantically for a suitable vehicle ferry. Such a vessel was finally found in May 1940 – appropriately named the *Hope*, built at Alloa in 1905 for use across the Forth. Originally a passenger ship, she had been adapted and ramps added and could carry a single lorry. She had been redundant since the opening of the Kincardine Bridge in 1936.

The *Hope*, however, proved mechanically unreliable and was eventually displaced by the *St Mawes*, built in 1917 by the St Mawes Company for their Cornwall ferry service between that village and Falmouth. She had been immediately requisitioned by the Admiralty and served out the Great War as a harbour launch. In 1920 she finally took up her ferry trade, only again to be called up on the outbreak of the Second World War. Clyde work then followed and, around 1947, the *St Mawes* became the latest Kessock ferry, adapted to carry five cars. Her Highland career was brief and she was broken up in 1951.

The *St Valery* was another passenger-only craft which ran alongside both the *Hope* and the *St Mawes* and served until the mid fifties. Meanwhile there was the first talk of a Kessock Bridge, as the 1948 Scottish Ferries Review reported that the current service was inadequate and a new, purpose-built car ferry should be commissioned. Someday, it mentioned in passing, a bridge would eventually be required. But post war public finances were so desperate that such a prospect seemed remote.

So finally a dedicated vehicle ferry was ordered from James Lamont & Co. Ltd of Port Glasgow. Launched in 1951 as the *Eilean Dubh* ('Black Isle'), the side-loading craft could carry eight cars on a fixed vehicle deck, had her wheelhouse forward and covered passenger accommodation aft. A small deck-turntable was located amidships, which the crew used to help manoeuvre cars and make maximum use of the available space. As the actual car deck did not rotate, the *Eilean Dubh* is not classed as a turntable ferry.

Deck-turntables were used for similar assistance on the large hoist-loading ferries subsequently built for Clyde and Hebridean services and on the early roll on – roll off cross-Channel vessels and were besides installed – though seldom used, and later removed – on the eight 'Small Island Class' bow loaders built for Caledonian MacBrayne in the 1970s. The similar, though tiny, *Cromarty Rose* on the Cromarty to Nigg crossing also boasted one, as did the two bow loaders built for the Western Isles Islands Council in the early 1980s.

The *Eilean Dubh* was supported by the *St Valery* at peak periods but she could not carry vehicles. In January 1953 the *Eilean Dubh* suffered a breakdown and, while the *St Valery* continued to offer a passenger service, cars had to make a 20-mile detour by Muir of Ord and Beauly. That same week, aptly, the Ministry of Transport approved the construction of an additional Kessock ferry, costing £7,985.

The *Inbhir-Nis* ('Inverness') was delivered from James Noble (Boatbuilders) Ltd of Fraserburgh in 1953 and was the only turntable ferry ever built for Kessock, able to carry four large cars and certificated for seventy-five passengers. She bore little resemblance to the yard's other turntable products. One obvious influence was the new *Portree* at Kyleakin – especially the substantial passenger saloon and the enclosed, twin steering-positions – but she had a mighty foremast and unusually high freeboard. She was besides the only turntable ferry ever built with fixed passenger gangways, lowered at berthing from saloon to slip. Compared to all the other crossings in this book, Kessock was unusual for heavy, pedestrian commuter traffic and this design-feature reflected that as did the 1953 timetable which showed the service running on weekdays on a half-hourly basis, from 07.30 to 22.30.

In summer there was also a limited Sunday roster. Some were later puzzled when Ross and Cromarty County Council publicly supported a local protest against the Caledonian Steam Packet Co. Ltd's determination, at Kyleakin, to force Sunday sailings on the Isle of Skye. By then Sabbath ferries were firmly established on the Beauly Firth on a service part owned by the selfsame council.

Car traffic pitilessly increased but local residents never really took to the *Inbhir-Nis* and, in October

1961, the Kessock Ferry Joint Committee pressed the respective local authorities for a new ferry - a 300-passenger, 20-car vessel. Meanwhile, the local manager – Captain R G Michie - approached Denny Bros. Ltd asking if a hovercraft might suit the route. The Dumbarton yard pointed out that their craft were still in the experimental stage.

Disgruntled with Denny's reply, in July 1962 the Kessock Ferry Committee sought the Scottish Home and Health Department for counsel about a putative hovercraft for fourteen to twenty cars and a hundred passengers. The crushingly sensible reply was not what they wanted to hear; the passage was far too short for one of the required size to be used at its full potential. Nor had the Committee evidently given any thought to the intolerable noise-nuisance for local residents. A few years later, there were indeed hovercraft ventures on the Clyde – firstly by Clyde Hover Ferries and then, with a chartered craft, by the CSP. They were not a success.

On 12th July 1964, caught unexpectedly by the flood tide at low water, the *Inbhir-Nis* smashed into the unyielding stone of the North Kessock slip. She was taken immediately to Inverness harbour and beached at low tide where workmen repaired a hole two feet long and six inches wide.

Some 35,000 vehicles were carried in June, July and August 1965 alone and, that September, subsidy for the operation of the ferry was sought from the Secretary of State for Scotland. This was refused as fares, it was pointed out, had not risen since 1954. A hike now would boost revenue and reduce the operating loss. Meanwhile, and at a cost of £95,000, a new and much larger car ferry had been ordered from the Berwick Shipyard.

The *Rosehaugh* was duly launched, at Berwick-

The side loading *Eilean Dubh* was the first car ferry to be built for the Kessock crossing and remained on station until the opening of the bridge in 1982.

upon-Tweed, in October 1966 – sideways, at full tide as she was too big to be sent down the slip - and was in service at Kessock by year's end. She was of even odder appearance than her predecessors with a bull-nose and double-ended with four corner-loading ramps and all the passenger accommodation down one side. However, she had powerful engines and with her Voith-Schneider units, a first for any Scottish car ferry, she was exceptionally manoeuvrable. She was a clear design influence on the big new ferries for Kyleakin several years later and gave many years of reliable service, firstly at Kessock and latterly (and indeed for longer) at Corran, and remains in private operation to this day. A rare lapse fell on Tuesday 9th February 1972, when she grounded in the River Ness and the aging *Eilean Dubh* had to deputise until she was returned to service.

The *Inbhir-Nis* completed her Kessock duty on the arrival of the *Rosehaugh* and was sold two years later to Thomas Jack & Co. Ltd of Larne, Northern Ireland. Very soon afterwards she passed to Colin M Hughes (North Highland Charters) of Foyers, Loch Ness and was operating across the Cromarty Firth between Nigg and Cromarty on charter to Brown & Root Wimpey, operating three or four round trips each day. Unfortunately her lack of passenger certificate proved to be her downfall and she completed service at the end of July 1972 later being noted on the slipway at Thornbush, Inverness minus her turntable. Her final fate remains obscure.

In 1975, following the reorganisation of Scottish local government, the ferry operations were transferred to Highland Regional Council. The opening of the Ballachulish road bridge closed the ferry there and the steel-hulled *Glenachulish* – as we have noted - was acquired for £15,000 by the Highland Regional Council. She was still only six years old and spent the next few years as a spare and relief vessel – annually at Kylesku, rather less frequently at Corran, but chiefly at Kessock, despite her limited capacity for cars and entire lack of covered passenger accommodation. She retained her bright, red and green Ballachulish livery to the last for these duties, although latterly with an all-green wheelhouse. Most of the time she simply lay at Muirtown Basin. For some desperate days in November 1979, when the

Rosehaugh was away for annual overhaul and the *Eilean* Dubh had suffered a major breakdown, the tough little vessel maintained the Kessock service single-handed.

Construction of a bridge – at last recognised as vital for the regional economy – had already been sanctioned although the span took shape on the other side of Inverness, from reclaimed land at Longman. The Kessock Bridge, of stayed design and specially strengthened against earthquakes as it crosses the Great Glen Fault, was finally opened by The Queen on 19th July 1982. The last normal sailings ran the previous day, with both vessels (though not the wee *Glenachulish*) offering special farewell trips on the same day. This was a momentous Highland occasion. For the first time, people living on the Black Isle could quickly reach Inverness at any time of the day or night and access for the emergency services and Raigmore Hospital was far quicker than in the past. Subsequent bridging of the Dornoch Firth shortened still further the journey to the far north by the A9 and in the decades since thousands of new homes have been built for Inverness commuters, north of the Firth.

For now, drivers queued all night to be amongst the first to cross the bridge a little upstream and the *Eilean Dubh* operated over thirty return trips carrying 1,152 exuberant passengers. Also offered was an excursion where passengers crossed by ferry one way and returned by bus over the bridge for £1. The *Rosehaugh* saw one final crossing to exchange commemorative scrolls between the Kessock communities before both she and the *Eilean Dubh* retired to Inverness Harbour awaiting their fate. The relief vessel *Glenachulish* was also laid up and for sale. By May 1983 she belonged to Murdo MacKenzie of Glenelg and was the new Kylerhea ferry.

The *Eilean Dubh* was sold on to Macdonald Ferries and used for local salvage and support work as well as supplying the oil rigs of the Cromarty Firth. She was eventually scrapped at Invergordon.

The *Rosehaugh* was transferred to the Corran ferry, and after her sale in 2001 – also to MacDonald Ferries - she returned to the east coast, where she was adapted for similar employment to her late sister. She sails still.

A quiet summer scene at Kyleakin with the *Moil* of 1936 alongside.

KYLEAKIN – Loch Alsh (Kyle of Lochalsh to Kyleakin, Skye on A87)

The straits of Kyleakin, some 500 yards wide, strewn with reefs and islands and exposed to strong, mountain-funnelled winds, are named after King Haakon IV of Norway, whose defeat at the 1263 Battle of Largs ended that nation's sovereignty over the Hebrides. Kyleakin is still overlooked by the crumbling Castle Moil and local tradition remembers one 'Saucy Mary' – an assertive Norse lady who strung a great chain over the narrows, to exact toll from any vessel seeking passage.

Although neither the oldest nor shortest crossing to Skye – it yields on both points to Kylerhea – the passage was long of local importance. That travelling cleric, Martin Martin, notes a ferry at Kyleakin in 1695 but it was the second decade of the nineteenth century before roads were built (under the direction of Thomas Telford) to Kyle of Lochalsh from Fort Augustus – via the Dornie ferry – and from Dingwall in the north, by the ferry at Strome. The first effective jetties were also built at Kyle and Kyleakin.

From the extension of the Inverness railway to Kyle of Lochalsh, in 1897 – it had reached Strome in 1870 – the Kyleakin crossing became rapidly the most convenient, in particular for motorists after the opening of the Dornie Bridge in 1940. Kyle of Lochalsh besides superseded Strome as the main port for MacBrayne services to Raasay, Portree, Harris and Stornoway, linking all to Inverness by rail and, from 1905, with an additional dogleg south by Kylerhea and the Sound of Sleat to Mallaig where the new West Highland Railway furnished direct connection to Fort William and Glasgow.

The first purpose-built car ferry was introduced in 1928 and the service was developed under the aegis of the London, Midland and Scottish Railway, first leased to the operation of David MacBrayne Ltd (in which the LMS held a 50% share) and from 1940 and thereafter by the Caledonian Steam Packet Co. Ltd, under assorted names from railway nationalisation in

1948 but resuming its own in 1957. With the creation of the Scottish Transport Group in 1969, bringing MacBraynes and the CSP together under wholly State-owned and Scottish control, MacBraynes yielded all their Clyde operations to the CSP. Gourock though, kept firm control of its solitary West Highland outpost, the Kyleakin ferry – not least because it was a veritable goldmine – until the consolidation of all car ferry and excursion-steamer operations in the new Caledonian MacBrayne Ltd, from 1st January 1973.

It had begun modestly. By the Great War, cars were borne over to Kyleakin by rowing boat, secured aboard using chocks and tied with ropes through the wheel spokes. No car was ever accidentally lost but on at least one occasion a vehicle was deliberately tipped overboard to save the ferry from capsizing. The first powered vessel appeared in 1914, a nameless motor-launch for passengers only. She was replaced in 1916 by a similar and likewise anonymous craft from Oban and 1918 brought the first named vessel, the launch *Kyle*. None of these motor boats toted turntables or carried cars but instead, they towed vehicles across by barge, as had been done successfully and safely on the Solent to the Isle of Wight for many years.

The *Kyle* was joined in 1923 by another launch, the *Skye*. The *Skye* allowed passengers to cross in more comfort than the *Kyle*, and could also tow a car-carrying barge. It may have been around this time the *Kyle* acquired what resembled a turntable platform athwart – but this was fixed and immovable. She could thus convey a single vehicle, but had to berth at specific sides of each slip so that the driver did not need to reverse. Photographs suggest she tied up port-to at Kyle and starboard-to at Kyleakin.

Real turntable ferries had long proved their worth elsewhere and 1928 saw the first built for the crossing. Her arrival neatly coincided with Skye's first timetabled bus service, from Portree via Broadford to Kyleakin where it connected with the Inverness train. The timber-hulled *Kyleakin* (I) could carry one car. She proved slightly underpowered and slightly too small and just three years later in 1931, she was re-engined, and lengthened a little to allow the carriage of two cars or one lorry. The year 1936 brought the 2-car, wooden *Moil* after which the motorboat *Kyle* was

disposed of in 1938. She seems to have been broken up in 1940. 1942 saw the commissioning of the first steel-hulled turntable ferry anywhere, the 2-car *Cuillin*, built by Denny Bros of Dumbarton. 1950 brought another, second-hand motor launch, the *Coruisk* (I), built in 1947 as the *Silver Grid* and with roomy passenger accommodation. The redundant *Skye* was sold that same year to a new owner in Greenock for use as a pleasure-boat.

Assorted matters of politics and practicalities beset operation of the Kyleakin ferry in these early years. In 1937 a Portree minister – the Rev'd John MacLeay – petitioned Inverness County Council to take charge of the service and place a 'modern, commodious ferryboat' on the crossing. The Chairman ruled this

Above: An earlier view at Kyleakin with what is believed to be the *Kyle* loading her single vehicle for Kyle of Lochalsh.

Left: The **Cuillin** (left) is almost ready to depart as sister craft **Moil** discharges on the other side of the slipway at Kyle of Lochalsh.

Top left: An unidentified ferry (the *Moil*, *Cuillin* or *Lochalsh* (I)) hurries away from Lochalsh in about 1951.

Centre left: The *Portree* (I) disembarks a Rolls Royce at Kyleakin.

Bottom Left: Having recently entered service, the *Lochalsh* (II) is seen arriving at Lochalsh in June 1957. *(Falkirk Museums)*

Above: The *Cuillin*, the passenger launch *Coruisk* (I) and MacBrayne's *Loch Seaforth* at Lochalsh during the early 1950s. *(Brian Maxted collection)*

Below: The *Portree* (I) alongside at Kyleakin.

incompetent as under the Piers, Harbours and Ferries Act a local authority could not take charge of a ferry from a railway company. Instead, they made complaint to the Secretary of State for Scotland and the Ministry of Transport.

Until 1938 when the Kyleakin slipway was extended by forty feet, the operation of the ferry was frequently disrupted by low tides. A sailing or row boat could simply run up the beach but the motorised craft with vulnerable propellers, could not. The pier works though, were briefly halted by village fishermen, anxious that the much-lengthened jetty would imperil future entry to their little port at night. A Fishery Protection Board cruiser duly arrived and after taking assorted soundings and bearings, marked out a safe channel for them. The new slipway could then be completed.

There were occasional mishaps. Early on 8th September 1928, the local minister and his wife were in their little Jowett, in the queue of vehicles at Kyle waiting to cross. 'The car in front of us was a two-seater driven by a lady who appeared to be travelling

The passenger launch *Skye* leaves Lochalsh as the *Kyleakin* (I) is pushed away from the slip in order to deliver her single vehicle to Kyleakin. The ferry was lengthened in 1931 after which she could carry two cars. *(Brian Maxted collection)*

alone,' he later recorded in his diary. 'When her turn came she boarded the ferry boat without any difficulty but she must then have mishandled her gears for to our horror the car glided slowly on and then toppled into the sea, only the back part and the back portion of the hood remaining above water. Fortunately a small boat happened to be in the immediate neighbourhood and the lady was got out in wonderfully quick time. She was deadly pale but did not faint. She was imprisoned by the hood but very

The *Kyleakin* (I) approaches Kyle of Lochalsh with a queue of nine cars waiting to cross. This situation would scarcely improve throughout the following decades. *(Brian Maxted collection)*

Right: A Skye Transport Albion bus unloads at Kyleakin as the *Kyleakin* (I) of 1928 prepares to leave for the mainland.

Below: The *Broadford* (I) of 1953 alongside at Lochalsh. The ticket office is on the right. *(AE Glen/ Bruce Peter)*

fortunately her head was above water. Had the car not remained upright on its nose the consequences might have been very serious. It was pitiable to see her effects floating about in the water and her beautiful car in such a plight.' Three decades later, others would be far less fortunate.

Mr MacRae, minister of Kilmuir and Stenscholl in the north of the island, was shortly at full blown war with the LMS Railway when early in 1929 they announced plans for Sabbath railway excursions from Inverness to Kyle, with Sunday ferries to bear the trippers over. The minister duly established the 'Skye Sabbath Defence League' and over the next year

directed an effective campaign, winning overwhelming support locally and organising a boycott of all LMS services to and from Skye. Although train and ferry continued to run, the railway company lost a great deal of business and endured sustained, highly damaging publicity. On 6th November 1930 and in a strained letter, the LMS Vice-President wrote to the minister stating that Sunday train and ferry services would be abandoned if Mr MacRae would only put an end to all the agitation on Skye.

In the sort of far happier publicity the LMS could not have bought, on 12th September 1933 the Duke and Duchess of York not only visited Skye, but came via Kyleakin and posed for photographs with the ferry (and Castle Moil) as lovely backdrop. In December 1936, of course, the Duke would assume the Throne in the wake of the Abdication crisis.

The coming of the Second World War greatly boosted the Kyleakin service. Kyle itself became an important and busy naval base, which is no doubt why – despite the national emergency and heavy demand on shipyards – the new *Cuillin* was sanctioned by the authorities. The Kylerhea service obligingly ceased for the duration of hostilities and the Dornie bridge eased access to Lochalsh from the south. From 1945

onwards the tale is one of remorseless expansion, often ahead of the operators' ability to cope.

In that year the service was sustained by three 2-car turntable ferries – the *Kyleakin* (I), the *Moil* and the new *Cuillin* – and the launch *Skye* which was finally dethroned in 1950 by the *Coruisk* (I). But the service struggled to handle all the summer car traffic now offering. June 1951 saw another Denny Bros product, the *Lochalsh* (I) – another 2-car ferry and little more than a repeat of the *Cuillin*, though certificated for a hundred passengers (when not, presumably, carrying vehicles.) However the new *Portree* (I), delivered that October though not taking up her duties until 1952, was much more ambitious.

This Denny Bros vessel was twin-screw, much bigger, could carry four cars and had a spacious passenger saloon aft topped by two enclosed steering-positions, or as it was put at the time, a 'raised and split bridge'. She bore no mainmast but

had a strikingly large foremast at her bows and was certificated for a hundred passengers.

She was the first in a succession of turntable ferries at their most sophisticated and powerful, in Kyleakin service and the pre-war wooden ferries could now be disposed of. The *Kyleakin* (I) was bought by one W T Forsyth for what seems to have been a brief, failed venture at Kylerhea before she was destroyed by storm at Broadford in 1959. The *Moil* was simply transferred by the British Transport Commission – then legal owners and operators of the CSP and much else, including the nationalised railways - to their docks at Grangemouth. She was last noted on the Forth in 1968 and her final fate is unknown.

The success of the new *Portree* meant a fast order to Denny's for a repeat and the *Broadford* (I) was launched at Dumbarton in 1953, assuming Kyleakin service in 1954. She had neater lines than her slightly older sister with nicely flared bows, a lighter foremast

Above: The barge and dive vessel ***Portree II*** is presently based in Cornwall but was originally the first ***Portree*** of 1951.

Left: Alongside at Lochalsh, the ***Broadford*** (I) remained in service until 1966. *(AE Glen/ Bruce Peter)*

The *Broadford* (II) of 1966 was one of the route's first pair of side loaders. She is seen at Ryde (Isle of Wight) during the summer of 1987 when engaged on digging trenches for sewage pipes. *(John Hendy)*

Below left: The *Kyleakin* (II) was the route's last turntable ferry and entered service during 1960. This view shows the ample passenger lounge at her stern. *(AE Glen/ Bruce Peter)*
Below centre: The *Lochalsh* (II) of 1957 alongside at Kyleakin. *(AE Glen/ Bruce Peter)*
Below right: The *Lochalsh* (I) of 1951 as she is today, a retired workboat laid up at Nigg. *(Ron Stewart)*

and a dainty mainmast between the steering-positions. Both vessels had a curious ramp mechanism consisting of cables on a pulley, linked to a counterweight and the ramps were unusually short, leaning outwards at an unnerving angle when raised. Meanwhile, there was no more need for the *Cuillin* and later that year she was sold to one John Lee of Belfast then sold on further to the Newry Port and Harbour Trust for use as a workboat. She was still on the Registry nine years later.

In 1955, Sunday sailings returned although there was just one in either direction in connection with a

bus-excursion laid on by a London travel agency in association with Ian McRae, mine host at the Marine Hotel, Kyleakin. There was widespread anger on Skye and 5,000 residents signed a petition of protest in addition to hostility from the County Council. The Sabbath-breaking was not resumed in 1956. It should be made clear, now that the matter is historic and there is 7-day ferry service throughout the year, that local objection was only ever to regular commercial Sunday sailings. No one in the Hebrides ever opposed emergency ferry runs on that day to convey, say, a doctor to Scalpay or an ambulance to the mainland, or to bear families and perishable goods safely home after Saturday disruption by gales.

The wee *Lochalsh* (I) was renamed *Lochalsh II* to make her original name free for a successor days before the launch, in February 1957, of a new turntable ferry at the Ailsa yard in Troon. Though very similar in design and lines to the recent Denny ferries, the *Lochalsh* (II) was significantly longer and could carry six cars. Her ramps were also more substantial and secured by the standard, hinged counterweight mechanism. She was fitted out in just a few weeks and joined the Kyleakin fleet in April – significantly flying the CSP flag; that name (and the standard) had been revived after a decade of nationalisation. The *Lochalsh II* was retained that summer but when the three newer ships coped happily with all the traffic on offer, she was marked for disposal. In 1958 she was shunted to the British Transport Commission's canal operations – later the British Waterways Board – at Inverness where her turntable was removed and she acquired a crane,

serving for many years as a useful workboat on the Caledonian Canal. Around 1990 she was sold to Seaboard Marine Ltd and resold, in turn, to McRae Marine at Nigg who used her in connection with oil-terminal and fish farm duties. She was finally left on the beach where she sits to this day.

In April 1959 there was a dreadful tragedy at Kyleakin, which had some bearing on the future design of turntable ferries and shook the confidence of many in the design. The minister of Bracadale, the Rev'd Donald A MacLean, had accepted a lift to the mainland from a local woman. There were two other ladies in the back seat and an infant in arms. His host was a nervous driver and as they waited to cross to Kyle, she asked MacLean to take control of the car for boarding. He was unfamiliar with the gears and braking and he trundled aboard, straight along the deck, and banged into the opposite ramp. It should have been secured but it was not. It dropped, and the vehicle rolled straight overboard and sank rapidly in some four feet of water.

Appalled onlookers could see the desperate struggle and terror inside. The car's roof actually broke the waves. A crewman grabbed an axe, leapt in and somehow got on top of the vehicle. He then pounded frantically at the rear windscreen but the glass simply refused to give. MacLean somehow struggled out and survived, but the women and the baby all drowned. MacLean was in no way to blame for the accident but – and he had forty more years to live – he never really got over surviving; never really lived it down.

Most subsequent turntable ferries would be built with spring-braced ramps (with the additional security of a latch and, besides, a securing chain, all of which can be seen on the *Glenachulish* today.) But the widely publicised calamity did abiding damage and may have underpinned MacBrayne's reluctance to acquire the last Kyleakin turntable ferries twelve years later. A similar horror at Kylesku, in 1961, did not help.

A further *Kyleakin* (II) came on station in July 1960 becoming the final turntable ferry built for the route. The new Ailsa tender for the job had been accepted only in January and, with traffic continuing to swell, her arrival was most welcome. She closely resembled the second *Lochalsh* but can be distinguished in photographs by a subtle difference in the railing of her vehicle-deck, the ramp counterweights hinge on a broad bar at each corner, rather resembling a horizontal hockey-stick. The air-start mechanism of both Ailsa boats is also evident in pictures. A high-pressure canister painted vivid red, sat by the steering positions atop the saloon roof.

Yet still there was a mounting degree of summer congestion and in 1961, the slipways at both Kyle of Lochalsh and Kyleakin were upgraded so that Kyle could now accommodate three vessels simultaneously and Kyleakin two, thus enabling smooth 4-boat operation when required. From 1964 there was yet further pressure on the service after the first of the three big new MacBrayne car ferries, the *Hebrides* (II), began a wholly new service to Harris and North Uist and not from Kyle, but from Uig in the north of Skye. (The Uists were now linked by a causeway and a bridge, so at a stroke, and by this new vessel, almost

Below left: The *Portree* of 1951 alongside at Lochalsh as the *Broadford* of 1953 departs for Skye.

Below centre: The *Broadford* (II) off service (left) and the *Lochalsh* (II) at Kyleakin. (*AM Young*)

Below right: Renamed *Boreford*, the former *Broadford* (II) is seen in the Millbay Docks at Plymouth during July 1989. (*John Hendy*)

all the Outer Hebrides could enjoy drive-on travel to the mainland.) This not only drew many new tourists through the island but also lorry loads of freight. The second new ferry, the *Clansman* (IV) that summer started her own seasonal Skye service from Mallaig to Armadale and although she would spend winter relieving on other routes, the roads through Sleat and Morar remained dire and it did little to ease the swelling demand at Kyleakin.

Though seasonal Sunday sailings were introduced and maintained, in the teeth of great local anger, from June 1965, and by decade's end all year round, it made very little difference. That year also saw a disastrous change in livery. The Skye ferries had long followed the smart 'Caley' colouring on the Clyde – black hulls with red boot topping, silver railings, white superstructure and buff or yellow masts – although, at this date had not acquired the white waterline. A new scheme of 'monastral blue' was now imposed on all the CSP fleet, with chocolate boot topping and (for those ships that had them) red lions-rampant on funnels. This blue varies comically in hue in photographs – from near black to lurid to powdery – and showed up rust, scratches and knocks dreadfully. But it would remain until the advent of Scottish Transport Group control in 1969.

The *Kyleakin* (II) would be the last turntable ferry built for the crossing or, indeed for the CSP. What the route really needed was large corner-loading craft of the sort soon to be exemplified by the *Rosehaugh* at Kessock. But management had neither the imagination nor the funds, especially when they had to solicit every penny from distant British Rail bosses in London.

In the winter of 1964-65, the *Portree* (I) was renamed *Portree II* and, shortly afterwards, an odd-looking boat was launched by James Lamont & Co. Ltd at Port Glasgow. The new *Portree* (II) had a tiny wheelhouse for'ard and no covered passenger accommodation but could carry nine cars on her fixed main deck, side loaded by two long angle-ended ramps. These were manually operated and a central

The Cumbrae ferry **Largs** leaving Largs. The converted bow-loading vessel transferred there from the Kyleakin route in 1972 having entered service as the **Kyleakin** (II) in 1960. She ended her days in South Yemen.

deck-turntable helped crew in shunting cars about and making full use of the space. In short order, the *Broadford* (I) was redubbed the *Broadford II* and a new *Broadford* (II) was launched by the Port Glasgow yard in 1966, assuming Kyleakin service the following year. Her wheelhouse was, more conventionally at the stern, and had two high enclosed steering-positions. Later a tiny passenger-shelter was fitted. She had hydraulic ramps and the new *Portree* (II) was similarly equipped at her next overhaul.

The *Portree II* was sold to Irish interests for service on Strangford Lough. She only got as far as Belfast before being sold to the Orwell & Harwich Navigation Co Ltd. but they never used her, selling her on to the British Atomic Energy Authority, who converted the vessel to bow-loading and put her in private service across the River Alde between Orford and Orford Ness, the home of the Atomic Weapons Research Establishment. The *Portree II* was later re-engined with Perkins diesels to give her more power but her subsequent career is remarkably vague; since 2004 she has been in the service of Mojo Maritime who operate her as a works-barge and dive-support vessel and still named the *Portree II*, looking very good for sixty.

The *Broadford II* was sold in January 1967 to the Orwell & Harwich Navigation Co Ltd but they never collected her. She remained at Kyleakin for over a year, forlorn and rusting until March 1968, when she was sold to Marine Transport Ltd of Cobh, Ireland. In 1981 she was broken up.

In 1969 a fifth vessel joined the Kyleakin flotilla, the *Coruisk* (II). She was built to the same loading arrangements as the recent craft but by the Ailsa yard at Troon and was fitted with a large passenger saloon astern. Though her career would be widespread and colourful, she was not long destined to serve on the route for which she had been built. The new Scottish Transport Group saw no alternative to the Kyleakin bottleneck but total re-design and construction of new broad, steep end-loading slipways and the introduction of two very large double-ended ferries. With the new Strome by-pass nearing completion (the road finally opened in October 1970) they feared yet more pressure on the crossing.

For the first time in the history of either MacBraynes or the CSP, the new ships were ordered

The *Coruisk* (II) discharging at Cumbrae Slip in July 1976. Her career as a side-loader at Kyleakin was only to last two years.

off-Clyde, from the Newport Shipbuilding and Engineering Co. Ltd., Monmouthshire in Wales and it was no fault of the STG that things went horribly wrong. Both new ferries should have been ready for service by the spring of 1970 but were delayed, and delayed again, by parts-shortages, and of course, strikes. Meanwhile, the creation of the new slipways had left only one side-loading berth available at either side of the Kyleakin straits. The delays to traffic throughout 1970 were frightful. In desperation, an overnight 24-hour service was introduced and the new boat nearest completion – the *Kyleakin* (III) was finally towed to the Clyde for fitting out. She eventually took up service in September 1970, after Kyleakin crewmen had been trained on a similar vessel at Strangford Lough, although not without teething-troubles. It was almost a year before the new *Lochalsh* (III) could join her, in August 1971. She was identical save for her fabulously elaborate masts and the two vessels not only both bore white waterlines but had their metal decking painted MacBrayne-style, in green.

Able to carry 28 cars apiece with Voith-Schneider propulsion and no need to make fast at slips, the new craft drew some influence in appearance from the *Rosehaugh* at Kessock and once they had settled down, proved to be a great success: it would be the mid 1980s before Kyleakin was once more a company headache.

Meanwhile, the Scottish Transport Group had to find a new role for five relatively new car ferries. In the event the three newest were all, within two years, simply converted to bow loading and transferred to service on the Clyde. The *Portree* (II) dramatically altered in appearance, took up Rhubodach-Colintraive service across the Kyles of Bute in April 1970. A year later, likewise rebuilt, the *Broadford* (II) joined her. They would remain on that station (with very occasional assistance at Cumbrae) until October 1986 when they yielded to the new 12-car double-ended ferry *Loch Striven*. Both then retired to Rothesay before, on 1st November they were bought by Mr Terry Hooper, of Sandbank on the Holy Loch, who collected them three days later. For some time he used them to supply US Navy vessels moored in the loch. In 1987 the *Broadford* (II) was sold for work at Ryde on the Isle of Wight, where she glamorously

assisted in the digging of an offshore trench for a new sewage pipe. By the following January she belonged to Divemex Ltd of Powys, who had meanly renamed her *Boreford* but by the end of 2000 she was back on the Clyde – apparently based at Renfrew - as a workboat named *Broadford Bay*. She seems to have been demolished around 2005. As for the former *Portree* (II), Hooper finally sold her off as a mooring and she can presently be seen afloat at Sandbank as a stripped but serviceable pontoon.

The new *Coruisk* (II) saw little regular Kyleakin service after the arrival of the *Kyleakin* (III). She had been early marked for a new role and soon after the delivery of the *Lochalsh* (III), after only two years service at Kyle, she was converted from a side to a bow loader for the Largs to Great Cumbrae service in September 1971, after spending the summer as spare at Kyle. At Troon whilst Ailsa's men converted her to bow loading operation, slipways were built at Largs

The **Portree** (I) alongside at Lochalsh while in the background adjacent to the railway station are MacBrayne's **Loch Seaforth** and the small **Loch Toscaig**.

and almost directly opposite on the shores of Great Cumbrae. The rebuilt *Coruisk* (II) took up this new service on 11th March 1972, able to load nine cars but, with her saloon extended a little forward beyond the steering-positions, somehow spoiled in appearance. When the new purpose-built and much bigger *Isle of Cumbrae* was commissioned for the route in April 1977, she then enjoyed nine exciting years on general relief duties, serving frequently at Cumbrae and Rhubodach but also at Lismore, Kyleakin, Raasay and regularly at Scalpay. On the arrival of the first of four new 'Loch Class' double enders in 1986, the 1969 ferry was offered for sale. She was bought by Euroyachts Ltd of Glasgow in September 1986 and sold on the following year, to a private buyer in Penzance. Her career since is yet to be ascertained.

As for the two turntable ferries at Kyleakin, STG management had casually assumed that MacBraynes would find some use for them. In fact, David MacBrayne Ltd – as Iain C Macarthur has detailed – were less than eager, deeming turntable craft old-fashioned and unable to handle very long, very heavy loads. In April 1970, though, the *Kyleakin II* (both had been renamed that year, for the sake of the new vessels) relieved on the Scalpay-Kyles Scalpay station and, a year later, the *Lochalsh II* undertook the same duty. She would remain there and, in October 1971 after major refit and slight modification to her ramps, was renamed *Scalpay* (II) and gave half a decade's service. Redundant from January 1977, she relieved briefly on charter at Corran that July. After prolonged lay-up first at Lochaline and then at Shandon on the Gareloch, the derelict ferry was in November 1979 sold for just £200 to the Ardmaleish Boatbuilding Co. Ltd, Port Bannatyne, Bute. They cannibalised her for spare parts and put the stripped pontoon to work in assorted Ayrshire harbours. She was seen at Ardrossan and Troon and last noted, in Ayr, late in 1988.

Her younger sister had a narrow squeak: by late 1971 she was in dreadful condition at Kyleakin and out of certificate, unable to assist in Christmas 1971 emergency when the *Lochalsh* (III) was blown across the end-loading slip at Kyle and the *Kyleakin* (III) was away for overhaul. The CSP were reduced to chartering the *Glen Mallie* from Kylerhea on Boxing

Day, to operate alongside a chartered passenger launch to maintain the service. She remained there until the *Kyleakin* (III) returned.

The Glen Mallie returned to the Kyleakin route in 1972 for one day; 26th November. The *Lochalsh* (III) was in Stornoway for a refit and the *Kyleakin* (III) was operating alone. She suffered a minor breakdown which put her out of service. Thus *Glen Mallie*, not even a Caledonian Steam Packet vessel, became the last turntable ferry to operate from Kyle of Lochash to Kyleakin. The CSP learned from their mistake and during every subsequent overhaul period a standby vessel was brought to Kyleakin to assist the remaining drive through ship.

But the *Kyleakin II* would fight another day. Such was the impact of the *Coruisk* (II) at Cumbrae and so rapidly did traffic build up, that in May her elder sister was towed to the Clyde for appropriate reconstruction. She emerged as the *Largs*, a 9-car bow loading ferry of quite neat lines and joined the *Coruisk* (II) in July 1972. She likewise followed her into a relief role from the summer of 1977, but largely as back-up at Cumbrae (with occasional help at the Kyles of Bute) and never served out of the Firth of Clyde. She gave her last CalMac sailings on 26th September 1983 and then retired to the East India harbour at Greenock. She was later acquired by the Ardmaleish yard on Bute and several years later in 1987, left British waters - freighted aboard a cargo-ship for South Yemen.

The last years of the Kyleakin ferry may be briefly told. In February 1971 the northern side-loading slipway at Lochalsh was demolished at the cost of £900 as it had proved to be a hazard to the new ferries. By 14th August the two ships respectively (and

Left: Flanked by the passenger vessel **Skye** and the turntable ferry **Kyleakin** (I), Their Royal Highnesses the Duke and Duchess of York are welcomed at Kyleakin on the occasion of their visit in September 1933.

Below: The **Lochalsh** (II) approaches Lochalsh in September 1966.
(David Parsons)

Below: The distant *Portree* (I) and the **Lochalsh** (II) are seen loading at the double slipways at Lochalsh. *(Brian Maxted collection)*

the *Lochalsh* had barely started) had already carried more cars than the crossing had borne in the whole of 1970. Each winter or spring, they were regularly overhauled at Fleming's yard on Goat Island, Stornoway, at first under tow by the last MacBrayne cargo-boat, the Glasgow-Stornoway vessel *Loch Carron* but after her withdrawal in 1976 by their own power. (Their older namesakes had both crossed the Minch unescorted although they were much smaller, relative to their size, tougher and more powerful.) A small bow-loading ferry was usually stationed at Kyleakin for winter assistance and, from 1986 the *Isle of Cumbrae* or one of the 'Loch Class' ferries served.

A brief but entire strike by Kyleakin ferry crew – who were dismally paid – caused some tourist panic in July 1978. By 1980 the ferries lay overnight at new 'otter' moorings, purpose-built below Castle Moil, rather than alongside the local piers and where they were much more secure. There were occasional groundings, prangs and mishaps; in 1983, a young crewman was accidentally killed in the *Kyleakin*'s engine-room and several years later, she broke down on passage in rough conditions and drifted helplessly for what, to those on board, felt an inordinately long period until assistance arrived.

But in time, the big double-enders became victims

of their own success. The commissioning in May 1986 of a new and (for the first time) a drive-through roll-on-roll-off ship at Uig, the *Hebridean Isles*, once more invited yet further traffic through Skye and the Newport-built vessels, worked so hard, were getting on, breaking down more and more frequently. Once again, by the late 1980s there were long queues waiting to cross. It was only when a controversial new toll-bridge for Skye was approved by the Scottish Office that Caledonian MacBrayne were allowed to commission two new 36-car drive-through ferries. Both built by Ferguson's of Port Glasgow, the *Loch Dunvegan* (II) took up service in May 1991 and the oddly named *Loch Fyne* (II) in September. Had CalMac began a permanent 24-hour service even five years earlier, and with at least one new ferry, then the Skye Bridge might never have been built at all.

The redundant craft were sold off to new careers in County Cork, in the Republic of Ireland. The *Kyleakin* (III) – (now the *Carrigaloe*) and the former *Lochalsh* (III) (now the *Glenbrook)* continue, over two decades later to carry passengers and vehicles on the 4-minute crossing of Cobh harbour – and, indeed, have by 2013 served longer in Ireland than at Kyleakin.

The Skye Bridge opened to traffic amidst much ill-feeling, at 14.00 on 16th October 1995 but the government of the day had forbidden CalMac to continue their car ferry service in competition. There was much sabre-rattling talk locally of running one privately but no suitable vessel could be found, and most of the bridge's vocal enemies were much keener on demonstrations. In any event construction soon afterwards, of the Kyle Prospect buried the surviving side-loading slip and greatly reduced the usefulness of the later terminal. A small passenger-only vessel did provide a desultory service to Kyleakin in the summer of 1996 but this was not continued.

CalMac were forbidden to redeploy the final Skye ferries until the change of government in May 1997. They were then restored to service, after eighteen months of somewhat leisurely efforts to sell them off. The *Loch Dunvegan* was settled on the Rhubodach-Colintraive crossing, despite her vast capacity and the *Loch Fyne* assumed the Lochaline-Fishnish crossing to Mull. The hefty tolls on the Skye Bridge were finally abolished on 21st December 2004.

KYLERHEA – Kylerhea (Glenelg to Kylerhea, Skye)

'Despite occasional reports of its closure,' John Prebble recorded thirty years ago, 'there is still a summer car-ferry between Glenelg and Skye and it is a humbling experience to watch Murdo MacKenzie's skill at the wheel of the little *Glen Mallie*. The arc of the boat's crossing, dwarfed by blue and silent hills, almost doubles the breadth of the Sound at this point. The distance is no more than five hundred yards, but too wide, one might think, for the Fingalians who decided to vault it on their spears, hurrying to defend their homes in Glenelg. They were mythological giants, however, and all succeeded, except one called Reath, who was drowned when his spear broke. He is remembered by the name given to the narrows – Kyle Rhea – unless one prefers to believe that it means the Strait of the Current, for the tides here are the swiftest on the coast...'

The shortest crossing from the mainland to the Isle of Skye is also the oldest, though not even before the Skye Bridge opened in 1995, the most convenient. The

This 1936 view of the Glenelg slipway shows the route's premier vessel *Kylerhea* loading an Armstrong Siddeley. The same vehicle crossed more recently on board the *Glenachulish*. (Michael Gardner)

Kylerhea narrows are reached by ancient and precipitate drove-roads, either side of the passage, with inordinately steep inclines especially on the Glenelg side and most vulnerable to winter snow. Prebble was right: the tide-race here is exceptionally strong – at times as fast as eight knots – and these are treacherous waters calling for keen local knowledge. The author and naturalist Gavin Maxwell, whose 'Camusfearna' lair was some miles south of Glenelg, twice ran his motor-

The *Queen of Glenalbyn* unloading at Glenelg in 1960. The former Ballachulish vessel's service on the route was to be all too brief. (George Carr)

launch aground here. The car ferry service, accordingly, has always been seasonal, has in recent years been deliberately marketed as a tourist attraction in its own right and its real importance is to the summer economy of Glenelg and Kylerhea themselves.

A ferry is known to have existed here since at least the 18th century; in 1722 General Wade's military road to Glenelg for access to the Bernera Barracks was constructed. The barracks were built to keep a watchful eye over the area following the 1719 Jacobite uprising. In 1821, the 'Colossus of Roads' himself – Thomas Telford – supervised the building of handsome stone slipways either side of the Kylerhea narrows.

One traveller, Edinburgh jurist and man of letters Lord Cockburn, was on 3rd September 1841 distinctly underwhelmed by his Kylerhea experience. 'Here we are in Skye, as proud as Columbus when he first landed in America,' he grumped to his diary that evening. 'This ferry, though boasted as the best in Skye, is detestable, at least for carriages, and as ill-conducted as possible. But what can a ferry be for carriages, where ours is only the third that has passed this year, and the object of the landlord of the ferry-house on each side is to detain instead of advancing the passenger, and where, when at last it is seen that they can carry it on no longer, the only machinery for putting the vehicle on board consists of dozens of lazy and very awkward Highlanders, all scolding in Erse, who almost lift it and throw it into the groaning boat...'

From the mid-eighteenth to mid-nineteenth century the crossing was kept busy besides transporting between 5,000 and 8,000 cattle across the narrows, en route to the great markets in the south. The animals were made to swim across at the slack tide with each having a rope placed around its mouth, which was in turn tied to the tail of the animal in front and in that manner they were navigated to the mainland. The 'Highland Drove' was re-enacted for a 1981 television documentary; but on that occasion the beasts were spared the swim.

The importance of the Kylerhea ferry was diminished once the railway reached Kyle of Lochalsh in 1897. Thereafter a passenger service was maintained until the boat was lost in a storm in 1915.

It was not until Wednesday 21st August 1935 that a ferry was re-established by Mr Lachlan Macinnes

The *Glenachulish* is seen approaching Kylerhea during a period of slack water in August 2012. (*John Hendy*)

with the help of the local minister, the Rev'd Thomas Murchison. The slipways had been repaired and improved and the new *Kylerhea* was pressed into service. She was a small wooden turntable ferry built by Messrs Stevenson & Asher (Boat Builders) Ltd of Banff. She could carry one large or two small cars on her deck.

And there was more competition than Kyleakin. In the same year a company was registered at Mallaig named ,'The Road to the Isles Ferries (Ltd)' whose vessel was a bow-loading craft, sailing in competition to the new venture at Glenelg. The ferry could convey between three and four cars on the route but, small, cumbersome and slow, she took fifty minutes to cross and so long delays were inevitable. It also cost £1 as opposed to the 8 shillings (40p) charged at both Glenelg and Kyleakin. This ill-conceived service only lasted a year and the company was wound up in 1937.

From 1936 the *Kylerhea* operated what has been pretty well the Glenelg-Kylerhea schedule ever since. She sailed at 09.00 from April until October excepting Sundays. Her day finished at half an hour before dusk, save between May and August when she sailed until 21.30. Until the advent of the Dornie bridge it should be remembered that in important respects this was a more convenient route to Skye than Kyleakin for the touring motorist. Vehicles heading for the Kyle of Lochalsh ferry had to cross another ferry before they even got to Kyle. If descending from the north, they had to brave Strome and, if from the south, Dornie.

A hazard of working the Glenelg crossing was, and remains, the ferocious tides with seiches and eddies and whirlpools to add to the excitement. As a result, even today, the ferry can rarely take a straight course between the two slips. She will head into the tide and 'ferry-glide' across the stream to reach the other side. The slipways have never been entirely adequate and at low water, the ferry often has to effect a 'T-bone' loading – berthing side-on to the very foot of the jetty – and, at extremely low tides, the service has to be suspended. There is little room for error in berthing at Glenelg, with serious and immovable rocks uncomfortably close to port. A ferry on the scale of the latter Corran turntable vessels could not operate here, and the greater 'updraw' from a twin-screw craft could also be risky in such shallow water.

The *Kylerhea* worked on the route until the outbreak of the Second World War, when fuel was in short supply and rationed and West Highland tourism simply ceased. (It was not just that folk had other things on their minds); thick with military bases, top-secret this and hush-hush that, most of the north-west became a 'Restricted Area', and even locals found freedom of movement rather limited.)

Laid up and idle for almost seven years, the *Kylerhea* resumed duty in 1946. However, completion of the Dornie Bridge during her absence had damaged her market as Kyle was now easier to reach, and by less demanding roads. It was now hard to operate the Kylerhea ferry at significant profit and so the service was consequently handed over to Lord MacDonald, laird of Sleat, and Ian Campbell. With so little traffic operating it proved unsustainable. The traffic was not busy enough to sustain the service and on the busiest day, the ferry carried only 28 cars. The *Kylerhea* was subsequently withdrawn and was eventually laid up at Inverie, on the north shore of Loch Nevis, where years later she sank at her moorings.

In 1951, the redundant Kyle of Lochalsh ferry *Kyleakin* (I) of 1928 was bought by one W T Forsyth, who used her to revive the Kylerhea ferry service. It is not sure for how many summers the *Kyleakin* (I) served

The **Glen Mallie** swings on the buoy off Kyleakin whilst out of service during February 1973. This reliable vessel was also to see service at Scalpay, Cuan and Kyleakin.
(John Hendy)

The *Appin Chief* abandoned on the shore at Glenelg prior to being scuttled. Her name board can be seen in the Glenelg Inn. *(Brian Maxted)*

built for a new MacBrayne car ferry. She was then abandoned on the shore.

Murdo MacKenzie had his own bright livery for the Glenelg ferries. The *Queen of Glenalbyn* was the first vessel he owned to have a grey hull. Later vessels added to this with a grey wheelhouse (*Appin Chief*'s was black for a time) and red ramps and A-framing with yellow railings. The *Glenachulish* was the last vessel to receive this livery, which she lost in 1991.

The *Appin Chief* was in turn joined by the 6-car *Glen Mallie* in 1969, after being displaced on Loch Leven by the new *Glenachulish*. Meanwhile, during the winter months the ships could be chartered. MacBrayne's new Scalpay ferry was first relieved in 1966 by a fishing-boat, but in 1967 the loss of their car ferry service caused much complaint. In 1968 and 1969 accordingly, the *Appin Chief* crossed the Minch to deputise. Under united STG control MacBraynes were able to borrow a Kyleakin turntable ferry in 1970 and 1971, but the *Glen Mallie* was again called on that October and relieved again in 1972, 1973, 1974 and 1975. She also assisted in emergency at Kyleakin in 1971 and 1972. Later, 1978 saw an unusual duty for the *Glen Mallie* as she headed south to Seil to cover for the *Belnahua* on the crossing to Luing for a few weeks.

Through 1969 and 1970, the delays at Kyleakin were so appalling that MacKenzie could profitably operate both his Kylerhea ferries at peak periods. But the advent of the big new double-enders at Kyle – the *Kyleakin* (III) took up service in September 1970 and her sister *Lochalsh* (III) the following August – transformed the situation. The new ferries each carried twenty-eight cars and up to two hundred passengers. The notorious queues evaporated. MacKenzie simply could not compete with that and it was not long before the *Appin Chief* was laid aside and beached in a village inlet, 'Hotel Bay.'

The 1970s were a lean time for the route and by late 1971 there were fears that the service would be closed. Traffic figures serve to illustrate the Glenelg route's plight: whereas in 1971, 14,525 vehicles had used the crossing, by 1975 this had dwindled to just 5,577. On 20th September 1975, the Glenelg crossing closed with MacKenzie struggling to meet the overhaul costs to Board of Trade certificate standards.

Despite much lobbying and some local clamour

at Kylerhea but we do know she was still running in 1953 as the AA road book for Scotland for that year states that a two-car turntable ferry was in continuous operation between 08.30 and 21.00 except for a lunch break between 13.00 and 14.00. By 1956, Forsyth had abandoned the trade and the *Kyleakin* (I), lying at Broadford, was lost in a storm during 1959.

In the late 1950s the sunken *Kylerhea* was located, raised and re-furbished by Murdo MacKenzie, a characterful Glenelg resident of enterprising bent. He re-engined her with an Ailsa Craig diesel engine and revived the Glenelg-Kylerhea service for the summer of 1959. She continued until the arrival of the spare, 1936 built Ballachulish ferry *Queen of Glen Albyn* in 1960. Thus passed the *Kylerhea* – the only ferry ever built expressly for the crossing.

The newcomer could carry two average-sized cars and it appears that on her arrival at Glenelg, the 'Glen Albyn' became one word on her hull and she was seen as the *Queen of Glenalbyn*.

All subsequent vessels at Glenelg were likewise redundant Ballachulish ferries. It was just a year later, in 1961, that the former Ballachulish ferry *Appin Chief* of 1955 was acquired. She doubled the capacity on the run as she carried four cars. The *Queen of Glenalbyn* ended her days at Craignure on Mull as a humble pontoon, used as staging as a new pier was the Highland Regional Council refused the Glenelg-Kylerhea service any subsidy, insisting these were for year-round rather than tourist routes. Nor were the Scottish Transport Users' Consultative Committee and the Highlands and Islands Development Board prepared to help. Fortunately there was another month's charter work at Scalpay and, when surveyed in May 1976, the costs of refit to certificate standard proved more lenient than feared. So the *Glen Mallie* did sail that summer and things were never as fraught again. Traffic picked up and a strike by Kyleakin ferrymen in the summer of 1978 made for very brisk business at Kylerhea.

When the new Kessock Bridge opened to traffic in July 1982, the Highland Regional Council had no further need of the ex-Ballachulish ferry *Glenachulish* and she had already been advertised for sale. Murdo MacKenzie bid successfully for the steel-hulled vessel and she assumed service at Kylerhea in May 1983 and in his livery. For the first time her wheelhouse was fully enclosed but unfortunately, this was done in cheap sterling-board. Earlier that year he had sold the *Glen Mallie*, to the Western Isles Islands Council who were under pressure to furnish safe arrangements for the transport of cattle to Vatersay. (A bull had drowned as it was swum from Barra, to much unpleasant publicity.) The veteran turntable ferry then gave two years of good service in this regard sailing from Vatersay to Castlebay, although she never took cars or passengers, but by late 1984 needed a costly refit. The Council deemed the expense prohibitive and she was abandoned in a tidal cove at Cornaig on Vatersay. The hulk was still afloat in 1990 but by 1997 had sunk and was rapidly disintegrating.

By the late 1980s, congestion was once again a problem at Kyleakin and the *Glenachulish* profited in turn. But Murdo MacKenzie was getting on in years. In 1988, he advertised his ferry, business and goodwill for sale, inviting bids around £55,000. Quite a few sought to acquire the *Glenachulish* but his determination to find a responsible buyer with the requisite seamanship delayed final disposal. There was no Glenelg-Kylerhea service at all in 1990 but later that year Roddy MacLeod, a jolly local fruiterer, who lived in Inverinate but was a native of Raasay, acquired the concern. The *Glenachulish*

resumed service in 1991, although in a rather drabber black-and-grey livery. The metal decking below the turntable was painted green and the bottom of her ramps were, as paint and whim permitted, painted red or vivid yellow. As MacLeod's operation prospered, he began shrewdly to market the *Glenachulish* herself – 'the last manually operated turntable ferry!' – as an attraction in her own right. Three others had still been in passenger service when Murdo MacKenzie had bought her in 1982 but by the summer of 1985, only she remained. In 1993 to some local controversy, Roddy MacLeod offered Sunday sailings for the first time and these have continued.

By the summer of 2005 and with a wary eye on Kyleakin, where the detested tolls had come off the new Skye Bridge, MacLeod was determined to retire and concentrate on his greengrocery. Mindful of Murdo MacKenzie's difficulties seven years earlier, though, he was eager to sell on reasonable terms to community ownership.

To make an involved tale boring, there was protracted panic when, after some disconcerting events, Glenelg residents voted down the chance to own and run their own ferry but the Isle of Skye Community Interest Company was formed in February 2006, drawing from the wider circle of Skye and Lochalsh. They initially leased the *Glenachulish* from

The last of the line: the **Glenachulish** moves astern from Glenelg during August 2012. *(John Hendy)*

MacLeod, until able to secure sufficient public monies to buy her outright and have been able besides to wage crew (including two qualified chargehands, Donald 'Donovan' MacDonald and Commander Quentin Banting), and a Chief Executive. The *Glenachulish* has sailed on, drawing healthy traffic despite immediate competition from a free Skye Bridge and the heavily subsidised Caledonian MacBrayne service from Mallaig to Armadale. Just part of the charm, apart from the seals, otters and dolphins regularly spotted or the coffee and souvenirs sold by an honesty-box system in a transplanted little lighthouse on the Glenelg side, or the ship herself and her jolly crew, is the long tradition of a resident ship's dog, and on occasion two dogs; at least when senior skipper Donnie 'Donovan' MacDonald is at the helm. The noble Border Collie, Burly, has been gathered unto his fathers but Nak reigns in his stead.

The Isle of Skye CIC has had besides to cope with the rocketing fuel costs since 2006, the ever more stringent (and not always self-evidently reasonable) demands of the Maritime and Coastal Agency to keep the *Glenachulish* in certificate, and the demands of maintaining what is now a 45-year old vessel in service – not least the difficulty in sourcing parts. (Her old chain-driven steering and, sadly, the attractive wheels had to be replaced some years ago by hydraulic gear, simply because the requisite chain in Imperial measurement was no longer available and the nearest fit in metric kept coming off.) They have to balance their obligations to the community with the demands of tourism and the need to recoup sufficient profit to keep the vessel in service. An additional difficulty is that, in law and as a Community Interest Company, they cannot borrow serious money.

This makes for some challenging marketing.

Crossing on the *Glenachulish* is not just taking the ferry to Skye. It is the experience of taking an historic vessel on an even more historic route. The slipways and berths for the vessel have been leased for a further 25 years, helping to secure the route for the future. A grant has also been approved for some important maintenance for the slips on both sides as well. The *Glenachulish* is usually refitted locally at Kishorn – where Commander Banting, enthusiast as well as junior skipper, lives - although she does occasionally cross the Minch to Stornoway for major work, where recently she had new ramps and a drive shaft fitted. (Such a voyage is a major undertaking – the turntable bolted and strapped down, the forward ramp lowered, and usually with an overnight stop at Gairloch, as the MCA does not like this low-profile vessel sailing at night. The worst thing for the crew is the cold; the best thing is the curry awaiting them from a resident Goan chef at Stornoway's County Hotel.)

An unexpected turn of events in December 2011 led to the *Glenachulish* reviving the service at Stromeferry for the first time in nearly 42 years. She operated there between Monday 16th January and Friday 23rd March 2012 due to a landslide on the A890 between Strathcarron and Strome and her duties are covered in much greater detail in our history of that crossing.

The ship is classed as a freight vessel, and as a result, carries a maximum of 12 passengers and up to six small cars and is the last of the long line of manually operated turntable ferries now in service. In 2018 *Glenachulish* will be 50 years old. To celebrate this she will be placed on the National Historic Ships Register; she has already been added to its Archive.

In January 2013 the *Glenachulish* lay at Mallaig for refit, including major reconditioning of her chortling Kelvin T-6 engine. The extra revenue from her recent, protracted service at Strome was most welcome in this regard as the new parts alone – an engine-block, pistons and liners, and more – cost some £23,000. The frequent swell at Strome had disturbed venerable sludge and sediment in her fuel tank and caused some mechanical difficulties (and a brief but embarrassing grounding). Towards the end of that Loch Carron service it was thoroughly cleaned. Unfortunately, plans to restore her to her pleasing Ballachulish livery for the 2013 season were on this occasion postponed, although the Company's chief executive, Clive Pearson, has confirmed that this will be done for the summer of 2014.

Her proud owners say that she is just as much a tourist attraction as a vital means of communication and for the 30,000 passengers that use her each year between Easter and mid-October, the excitement and experience of sampling a Scottish national treasure is most evident.

KYLESKU – Between Loch Cairnbawn and Loch Glendhu & Loch Glencoul (Unapool to Kylestrome on A894)

This, the northernmost turntable ferry crossing, was in wild and lovely west Sutherland across the narrows of Loch Cairnbawn – itself the confluence of two inner sea-lochs, Loch Glencoul and Loch Glendhu. Since the Great War like much of the West Highlands, it has become sadly depopulated and Sutherland generally has not been fortunate in its landlords who directed infamous evictions in the early nineteenth century. On a brighter note, the Second World War saw secret training here – from 1943 onwards in the heroic and unnerving operation of miniature submarines as the brave men of the XIIth Submarine Flotilla learned how to handle their 'X-Craft' and 'Chariot' vessels in these deep inlets. A dignified little monument remembers their heroism by the Kylesku Bridge today.

The ferry linked Unapool, in the parish of Assynt, to the south, with Kylestrome, in Eddrachillis to the north and the only alternative was a wearying 100-mile

detour by Lairg. There was never great pressure of tourist traffic and for most of its history the crossing could be adequately maintained by one vessel. Unlike most West Highland ferries at this period, there were Sunday sailings and for much of the twentieth century

Above: A pre-turntable ferry in operation during the 1920s.

Left: Another view of this unnamed vessel which was in service between about 1920 and 1950.
(Brian Maxted collection)

The Maid of Kylesku
remained in service until 1976
before being abandoned on
the nearby shore.

the Kylesku ferry was free.

A row-ferry operated across at Kylesku from the early 1800s to avoid the detour. The first motor-ferry on the route seems to have been introduced shortly after the Great War and operated only during the summer months. A yellow flag was flown from the slipways when the tide was too low to allow loading while a red flag was flown when the weather precluded sailing.

During the 1930s, the route was operated from mid-May until mid- October by - improbably - the Scottish Automobile Association, until in August 1949 it was assumed by Sutherland County Council who graciously abolished the fares. At this time the hours of operation were 09.00 until 21.00. There was an amended timetable in operation during the winter months, without Sunday sailings and with a shorter working day.

We know little of this first vehicle ferry, although surviving photographs depict what seems to be a turntable vessel designed so that the car deck could be rotated by 180 degrees so the vehicle faced the bow of the vessel. The boat then berthed bow on to the slips at either side to allow the vehicle to drive straight off. This design would not allow operation at extremes of the tide, hence the aforementioned flags.

It is thought that she survived until the advent of the first vessel we can confidently identify. We note that in 1951 the Sutherland County Council approached the Ballachulish Ferry Co. Ltd seeking to charter their ageing *Maid of Glencoe* (I) but were rebuffed.

Delivered in 1952, *The Maid of Kylesku* – most unusually, the definite article was part of the name – was a 4-car, timber-hulled, single-screw turntable ferry constructed by James Noble (Boatbuilders) Ltd of Fraserburgh, who by now had all but cornered the market in such craft. The influence of the *Garven* and the *Mamore* is obvious and she was painted a dark juniper-green, with dusty red decking and white railings. Her ramps were of a unique grated design, probably for lightness.

The Maid of Kylesku

could carry up to thirty passengers and was fitted with an exposed steering position aft.

Wheelhouses had yet to become standard and conditions for Kylesku ferry crew were tough. The assistant ferryman, for instance was expected to put in a 10-hour shift – and that for seven days a week during the summer. In 1953 *The Maid of Kylesku* sailed from 09.00 until 19.00 in the summer and from 09.00 until dusk in winter. In 1957, fortunately, a second assistant ferryman was employed making conditions a little more bearable. Every year more and more tourists crossed: in August 1957 alone, 2,536 cars crossed at Kylesku but with just the one vessel operating the route, the service was suspended during winter overhaul periods. In 1958 for example, there was no Kylesku operation between 16th and 29th March. (MacBraynes likewise did not provide a relief car ferry for Scalpay until the third year of that service.) By the following autumn though, a relief-vessel had been acquired in the form of the redundant 4-car Ballachulish ferry, the *Mamore* of 1951.

On 14th July 1961 there was a dreadful accident at Kylesku when a car rolled backwards from *The Maid of Kylesku*, over the bows and straight into some forty feet of water. Of the four tourists inside, three drowned. The vessel was taken off the crossing immediately, carefully surveyed and her certificate duly restored by the Board of Trade. The *Mamore* assumed the crossing in her absence and *The Maid of Kylesku* resumed service by September. Meanwhile the Procurator Fiscal directed an investigation, and a Fatal Accident Inquiry was subsequently held at Dornoch Sheriff Court, as the 'Northern Times' reported that October:

"A jury of four women and three men returned a formal verdict at an inquiry at Dornoch Sheriff Court last Tuesday into the tragic accident at Kylesku vehicular ferry, North West Sutherland, on July 14 last, when three persons lost their lives through drowning. Eleven witnesses were called.

It was indicated during the evidence that more stringent safety precautions were to be applied to all Scottish ferry boats in future. An announcement would be made very shortly regarding fresh regulations, said Mr Ernest Earnshaw, Ministry of Transport marine and ship surveyor.

After the Kylesku accident he had examined the ferryboat, Maid of Kylesku, and found it "perfectly satisfactory." No blame, he agreed, could be attached to the operators (Sutherland County Council).

Mr Earnshaw also described additional safety devices which had been introduced at Kylesku since the accident. Wooden wedges were placed under car wheels and a chain was placed across each ramp when they were in the up position and the boat was ready to leave the jetty. These were simple and effective safeguards.

Three holidaymakers were drowned in the accident. There was one survivor who was driving the car when it suddenly moved backwards on the ferry turntable and went through the ramps and sank in 40ft of water.

It was at least the third occasion that a car had boarded a turntable ferry and ended up in the sea, and the second when people had died."

In 1967, *The Maid of Kylesku* was dethroned by a large new vessel, once again from the Noble yard at Fraserburgh. The *Queen of Kylesku* was practically a repeat of their 1964 vessel for Corran, the *Gleann Mhor*. The vessel could squeeze on nine small cars, was certificated for passengers who enjoyed a small shelter, at main deck level and connecting her two elevated covered steering-positions. She had a dark green hull (it can look black in some photographs) with a red strip and a grey wheelhouse. The *Mamore* could now be disposed of. She is known to have been used in connection with the building of a new Lochinver pier that same year and was then simply abandoned

The Maid of Kylesku is seen in 1964. Her exposed steering position should be noted. *(David Yates)*

Above: A powerful 1970 view of the three-year old **Queen of Kylesku** which was a far more sophisticated craft than her predecessor. *(David Parsons)*

Below: Abandoned on the southern shore, **The Maid of Kylesku** is a reminder of Sutherland's ferry heritage. *(Brian Maxted)*

they drove and was strong enough and with sufficient overhead clearance to carry anything that could legally take the British roads. Unfortunately she was plagued with mechanical problems. The proprietor of the Kylesku Hotel would later claim that during her first six months in operation, she had managed only ten full days in service and the burden on her turntable sisters must have been considerable. The *Maid of Glencoul* – presumably under guarantee – had finally to be fitted with new engines, and practically overnight became a most reliable ferry; nearly forty years on, she sails still.

She brought two changes: a new and vivid livery (blue hull and white upperworks, with pale red metal decking) and, rather less diverting for locals, the first ferry charges since 1949. Single passage for a car was now £1. A few months later, in the summer of 1976 *The Maid of Kylesku* was offered for sale. A local fisherman snapped her up, removed her engine and left her high on the beach by the Unapool slip where she lies to this day. She was not so much a casualty of the grand new ferry's arrival as of her own advanced years and Highland Regional Council's purchase late in 1975, of the redundant *Glenachulish*, which spent a month or two at Kylesku every year to cover for annual overhauls. The 1967 *Queen of Kylesku* was retained to the end as the secondary ferry. It is unclear what arrangements were made for relief after the sale of the *Glenachulish* for a new career at Kylerhea in 1982. It is possible, though unlikely, that a spare Corran turntable ferry was sent north in 1983.

On 8th August 1984 The Queen opened the new and surprisingly attractive new road-bridge – a curved elegant construction which sat well in the landscape and won one or two notable awards – and there was an appropriate ceremony with local schoolchildren and the *Maid of Glencoul* was dressed overall. She was subsequently overhauled and modified for service at Corran and took up service there as principal vessel in 1985. With the arrival of a purpose-built and larger ferry in 2001, she stayed on as spare and relief ship. The *Queen of Kylesku* was acquired by the Tanera Mor fish farm, based on the largest of the Summer Isles in Loch Broom, renamed *Queen of Tanera*, and spent quite a few years as a workboat there. She has long lain derelict on the island's beach.

at the tidal mouth of the River Culag. *The Maid of Kylesku* was retained as relief and back-up vessel.

During June, July and August 1972, the Kylesku ferries carried some 42,000 cars and the County Surveyor declared that serious consideration must be given to the construction of a bridge. Meanwhile, the growing number of heavy commercial vehicles seeking passage to the far north called for a very different sort of vessel and tenders were invited by the new Highland Regional Council. A £239,000 order was duly laid with William McCrindle Ltd of Ardrossan.

The *Maid of Glencoul* was an 18-car corner-loading bull-nosed ferry, echoing the *Rosehaugh* at Kessock, with two diagonally opposed hydraulic ramps to load her single fixed vehicle-deck. She was certificated for 116 passengers and their covered accommodation was in a saloon the length of one side. She was steered from a covered wheelhouse on a central spanning bridge, with direct control of her engines and the cycloidal Voith-Schneider propulsion units

SCALPAY (Scalpay to Kyles Scalpay, Harris)

The history of the only turntable service in the Outer Isles was as brief as it was late.

The arrival of MacBrayne's new car ferry service from Uig to Tarbert and Lochmaddy in May 1964 had seen the demise of the 1930 mail boat *Lochmor*, which had served the Small Isles and the central Outer Hebrides from Mallaig and Kyle in an involved run twice a week, circumnavigating Skye in both directions. Following the introduction of revised services to Tarbert (Harris) in 1964, the island of Scalpay found itself without a ferry link. The new *Hebrides* (II) would not call there, although nearly half a century later we now know that her impact on the islands was epochal, greatly boosting tourism and ending, barely a decade later as road-haulage became the norm, MacBrayne's final cargo-boat runs.

Scalpay is a rocky, characterful landscape. When Charles Edward Stuart took shelter there weeks after the disaster of Culloden, it was occupied by only one family, that of the resident 'tacksman', or small renting farmer, who cared for the Prince bravely and with no mean patience until they managed to move him on. The island was only settled in the 1840s after vicious clearances elsewhere on Harris, and became rapidly overcrowded. Though affording wonderful views to Skye, the north-west Highland coast and the Outer Hebrides, it has very little workable land. Resourceful new residents looked fast to the sea and by the Second World War, were exceptionally skilled and successful fishermen in a place bustling with life and seething with children.

In the early 1960s only a handful owned cars and, although with a network of quite neat single-track roads, none were tarred.

Most Scalpay residents, of course, had boats and could come and go as they pleased to Tarbert. The fishing trade took her men regularly to Stornoway and elsewhere. Meanwhile, mails and visitors were conveyed on a rather informal basis by two fishing-boats, the *Catriona* and the *Morea* but more permanent arrangements were desirable, and MacBrayne management were soon in talks with Inverness County Council.

Seen alongside at Scalpay in September 1969, the **Scalpay** (I) was the former Ballachulish ferry **Maid of Glencoe** (II). *(Robin Love)*

On the latter's assurance that slipways and associated roadworks would be laid on, it was decided to provide a small car ferry over the narrow Scalpay Sound to the adjacent village on the Harris mainland, Kyles Scalpay. A vocal folk, the Scalpay residents made all sorts of noise; an early fear was that they might as a consequence lose their junior secondary school (in fact, it would survive until the demise of the ferry) and they insisted besides on a constant shuttle of buses from Kyles Scalpay to Tarbert.

A turntable ferry was then the conventional solution and through the 1960s second-hand tonnage was readily acquired as operations here and there upgraded to newer, usually bigger boats. With the delivery of the 6-car *Glen Loy* for Ballachulish service in 1964, the 1956 vessel *Maid of Glencoe* (II) became available and David MacBrayne Ltd bought her for £1,600. The 4-car timber-hulled single-screw ferry duly went to the yard of Timbacraft Ltd, Shandon, on the Gareloch, for an extensive refit, which included re-engining, and emerged in the Company's traditional livery for its small wooden craft - a bright red hull with white railings and detail and blue boot-topping. She was MacBrayne's first turntable ferry (they had for a few years operated those at Kyleakin, but never owned them) and the only car ferry ever painted thus in CalMac history.

The *Scalpay* duly took up her new duties on 10th May 1965. There was no formal timetable in the early years, the service merely being advertised as 'frequent' and pretty well to demand but there were runs to connect with early departures or late arrivals of the *Hebrides* and she worked roughly a 12-hour day. Passage itself took scarcely two minutes, the real chore being loading and unloading although it became apparent that the new slipways were rather narrow for comfort. In later years the first return crossing was dropped from the Wednesday afternoon roster, as the ferry usually made a run to Tarbert then to refuel. (The later bow loaders only needed to do this once a fortnight.) MacBraynes had their own diesel storage in a great tank behind their Tarbert pier office but since the conversion of the current *Hebrides* to burn heavy fuel oil several years ago; this eye-sore has been removed.

No Sunday service was ever run, although the

Scalpay (I) sailed as usual on Christmas Day 1965. From 1st January 1966 MacBraynes boats did not routinely operate on that holiday or at Christmas and it would be 1972 – to Mull, and against some local opposition – before they offered regular Sunday sailings anywhere. The Scalpay ferry and her crew did of course make emergency runs on Sundays, usually for the Tarbert ambulance or the local doctor. There was an unusual business arrangement, later adopted when the Raasay car ferry service began, but which management must later have regretted at Scalpay: the company supplied the vessel and covered the costs of her maintenance, her overhaul, her insurances and ship-depreciation, but the crew – unwaged and all members of the same close-knit MacSween family, soon known locally as 'The Ferries', sold the tickets and kept all the revenue. It is whispered that they did very well out of it over the next thirty-two years but they worked very hard, turned out cheerfully, especially when medical aid was urgently needed, were charm personified and kept their command in immaculate condition. It says something of the

Below: In June 1974, the *Scalpay* (II) (ex *Lochalsh* (II)) heads away from Tarbert (Harris) after her weekly call to take on bunkers. *(Lawrence Macduff)*

The **Scalpay** (I) at Scalpay in July 1968. She was condemned during her annual survey in 1971. *(Lawrence Macduff)*

Scalpay character that two objects were invariably in evidence in the ferry wheelhouse – a well-filled ashtray and a well-thumbed Bible.

Meanwhile, Scalpay roads were at last metalled, everyone rushed to buy a car and within a matter of months the buses scurrying to and from Kyles (it is pronounced locally, by the way, with two syllables) were for the most part empty. The provision was rapidly wound down, though school buses ran for the secondary children and in the late 1970s a shelter was built for them by the top of the Kyles slip. (This was demolished after cessation of the ferry service in 1997.)

The *Scalpay* (I) usually headed to Stornoway for refit and during her first annual overhaul period in October 1966, no one seems to have minded; the *Morea* and the *Catriona* resumed their duties. In 1967 though, the same arrangements were made and on this occasion there was great complaint at the lack of a car ferry. The Company listened and in the springs of 1968 and 1969 the *Appin Chief* was chartered from Kylerhea as the relief vessel. By 1970 MacBraynes were part of the wider Scottish Transport Group and in May that year the 1960 6-car *Kyleakin II* (she had just acquired the numeral, to clear her original name for her successor) proved a very successful substitute. Had the CSP anticipated the great difficulties they would face at Kyleakin that year – the *Portree* (II) now served on the Clyde, and the big new boats did not arrive on time – they might not have assented to the arrangement.

In April 1971 the *Scalpay* (I) was fifteen years old and due for her third 'quinquennial survey', under a Board of Trade regulation mandating especially close scrutiny of hull, frame and engines every five years. On this occasion the 1957 *Lochalsh II* (II) came from Kyle to cover for her. The quinquennial survey was most conveniently done by Board officials at Shandon on the Clyde and the ex-Ballachulish vessel was fast condemned, being in a dreadful state structurally and mechanically. With no obvious role elsewhere for the redundant Kyleakin turntable ferry, which proved no less successful on the Harris station, it was decided permanently to retain her at Scalpay. Her predecessor was taken over by Timbacraft Ltd, perhaps in lieu of the bill, and stripped to a pontoon, her engines and turntable being scrapped. It is most unlikely this survives.

The *Lochalsh II* (II) herself needed annual overhaul and a degree of refurbishment and, in mid-October, she too voyaged south to Shandon although with a happier ending. She was thoroughly refitted and angled ends were cut into her ramps for ease of loading and offloading on her narrow new slipways. Renamed *Scalpay* (II) she was transferred to the fleet of David MacBrayne Ltd from that of the Caledonian Steam Packet Co. Ltd. Her metal decking was painted in MacBrayne green, which had become standard since the advent of the 1964 car-carriers – it had hitherto been red or dark brown. Meanwhile, Scalpay was served under charter again, by the *Glen Mallie* of Kylerhea, until the ex-Skye ferry returned triumphantly in mid-December.

From 1st January 1973, the CSP was renamed Caledonian MacBrayne Ltd and took over the mass of the combined operations, the plan being that they would run all the routes that did not need subsidy (confidently expecting profitable car ferry services all over the place) and cross-subsidise the four surviving pleasure-steamers. Most of the combined fleet passed to the legal ownership of Caledonian MacBrayne Holdings Ltd. David MacBrayne Ltd was left as owner only of a handful of vessels on uneconomic routes or of obsolete character or directly subsidised and only one car ferry – the second *Scalpay*, no doubt reflecting the fiscal arrangements for her operation. She in fact remained registered with David MacBrayne Ltd for the rest of her career, although the 'Oil Shock' and economic woes of the 1970s evaporated any hopes of a profitable CalMac and the dual ownership was abandoned in 1980.

With greater capacity and twin-screw power, the *Scalpay* (II) proved a very good and useful little ship on her new station and proceeded to Stornoway each October, from 1972 to 1975, for survey and hull-cleaning when the invariable relief was the *Glen Mallie*.

But she was getting on. The crew always found her all-steel turntable heavy. Most of the craft detailed in this book had steel-framed turntables with wooden decking and on occasion, when it seized, the best expedient was simply to throw a bucket of seawater into the bearing. Though she seems only twice to have broken down in her Harris service (and could still sail, if in calm conditions only, on one engine), parts for her Gleniffer engines were growing hard to find. 'The Ferries' also found the air-start an awkward arrangement and it was much harder to obtain regular supplies of compressed air in the wilds of Harris than at the Kyle of Lochalsh railhead. She was (since the conversion of her younger sister for Largs-Cumbrae operation in 1972) now the only turntable ferry in the fleet and management increasingly resented the cost and bother of chartering a replacement. Dark politics began to centre on her. We cannot now ascertain if CalMac genuinely wanted to convert the Scalpay service to end loading or if they wanted shot of this service altogether but they began increasingly to demand new slipways and eventually did threaten to withdraw. A real fear must have been the general demise of turntable ferries everywhere and, by 1975 it was widely thought that MacKenzie's own Kylerhea operation might soon be history. How then could the Scalpay ferry be relieved?

In January 1974 a late Friday sailing was offered for the first time, to connect with the later sailings of the *Hebrides* from Uig on Skye.

In September 1974, the *Scalpay* (II) broke down and there was no car ferry service for some days. The call was made to Glenelg and Fleming's yard in Stornoway was booked for an early overhaul. Once again the *Glen Mallie* covered her absence until the errant *Scalpay* (II) returned on 25th November. That same month, Inverness County Council was approached for a subsidy to operate the service and permission to upgrade the slipways to allow the new 'Small Island Class' vessels to operate there. Gourock was firmly rebuffed.

A few weeks later at the New Year of 1975, the *Scalpay* (II) broke down again and ran on just one engine during calm conditions until she was repaired on 9th January. She was joined by an unnamed motor launch dropped off by MacBrayne's *Loch Carron*, which was to convey passengers if required. It was rarely used and lay rotting on the beach by the Scalpay slip until 1997 when it had to be removed to allow use of the ancillary berth for Edmund Nuttal Ltd's little landing-craft; the company was then erecting the new bridge – and baulked at the MacSween rates for passage.

The *Scalpay* (II) made it through the summer with no more incidents or breakdowns and retired to Stornoway as usual in October for refit with the *Glen Mallie* covering until her return in mid-November. Despite some alarm, the Kylerhea ferry did not in fact cease but 1975 did prove to be the *Glen Mallie's* last visit to Scalpay.

Back on the mainland the newly opened Ballachulish road bridge had made the last three turntable ferries there redundant. The *Glen Duror*, *Glen Loy* and *Glenachulish* could all carry six cars and the Chairman of the Ballachulish Ferry Co. Ltd, Cameron of Lochiel – who was also a county councillor – publicly suggested that the newly formed Western Islands Council snap them up. He suggested one could be the reserve vessel at Scalpay and the others might develop new car ferry crossings to Eriskay, or Berneray or Vatersay. In hindsight, it was a shrewd suggestion and, in direct operation by the new local authority and with so little heavy traffic braving the fraught local roads, turntable ferries could have served Scalpay perfectly well until the advent of the bridge. But the hint was not taken; the two older Ballachulish

Below: The *Scalpay* (II) at Scalpay in May 1972. Her ramps were modified before taking up her new service. *(Lawrence Macduff)*

ferries were all but exhausted and by 1976 it was obvious that the *Scalpay* (II)'s days were also numbered. Rather than taking charge themselves, the Western Isles Council agreed later that year to rebuild the slipways and meanwhile lay temporary ramps – one by the Scalpay terminal, where there was enough beach, and one at the end of Tarbert's Old Fishing Pier. There was no convenient site for one by the Kyles jetty.

During the building works the *Scalpay* (II) operated between Tarbert and Scalpay, a crossing of 20 minutes as opposed to her usual 3 minutes. In the circumstances she did not enjoy a Stornoway overhaul that year and instead a one-week extension was sought (and granted) on her passenger certificate from 4th January until 12th January 1977, just long enough for CalMac to despatch their 6-car 'Small Island Class' bow loading ferry, the *Morvern*. The old Skye ferry gave her last run on the evening of 12th January 1977. On the following day, the *Morvern* took up the new 20-minute passage to Tarbert and when time permitted, the *Scalpay* (II) was made fast in a remote tidal cove of the island's South Harbour.

But it was not – quite - the end. That summer an emergency arose at Corran and the Highland Regional Council desperately sought a turntable ferry - any turntable ferry. On 7th July, the *Scalpay* (II) was roused from her slumbers and sailed to Stornoway for a quick Board of Trade survey. After gaining a certificate she then – for the first time in years – sailed south on the 12th for Kyle of Lochalsh, her old home. The following day she continued round by the Sound of Sleat and the Sound of Mull and up Loch Linnhe to Ardgour to take up service at Corran on 14th July alongside the *Lochaber* on charter to the Highland Regional Council while the *Gleann Mhor* was detained at Crinan on a major refit. The old Skye and Scalpay veteran suffered a turntable breakdown on the 16th. She was able to resume service the next day and assisted intermittently until the *Gleann Mhor* arrived back in the first week of August. Then she developed mechanical problems and so the *Scalpay* (II) was again used until one of her own engines also failed (as it proved, permanently.) She was towed by the *Eigg* to Lochaline on 7th August and lay there moored alongside the *Morvern* which had been relieved at Scalpay by the *Kilbrannan* on 2nd June.

The vessel remained there until May 1978 when she was towed back to Shandon and cannibalised for spares for the *Largs*, ex *Kyleakin II*. In November 1979 she was purchased for just £200 by the Ardmaleish Boatbuilding Co of Bute who overhauled the *Largs* and, minus her turntable, and (by 1983) her steering-positions, the 1957 veteran finished her career as a barge on the Ayrshire coast. She was later noted at Ardrossan, Troon and Ayr. The hulk may still survive.

From late April the *Morvern* could use the reconstructed Kyles slip and in early June she was replaced on the Scalpay station by her elder sister, the *Kilbrannan* of 1972. She would serve the island until 1990, when she yielded in turn to the slightly larger, 7-car 'Small Island Class' ferry *Canna*, built in 1975. From 1983 a small slipway in Scalpay's North Harbour allowed occasional emergency service direct to Tarbert when whether conditions made the Sound somewhat intimidating and from 1986 the new linkspan at Tarbert could be used, and the 1976 slip was allowed to disintegrate. In the early years of end-loading operation the regular relief was the *Coruisk* (II) of 1969, another ex-Skye side loader converted to bow loading for Clyde service. Her Scalpay crew, though, found her dangerously underpowered and early in 1984, dashing to Tarbert with a medical emergency, deliberately ran her high ashore on the slip as the safest option in the conditions as they did not trust her English Electric engines to hold her to the hard. From her demise in 1986 the relief was usually the youngest of the 'Small Island Class' vessels, the *Raasay* of 1976. She was overhauled at Stornoway and could slot in this duty en route. The MacSweens disliked her shorter ramp and the clatter of her capped exhaust.

In February 1997 the *Rhum* of 1973 assumed the Scalpay service for its final months, arriving in shamefully battered and dirty condition. She made the final morning sailings, before the Scalpay Bridge was opened by the island's oldest resident – 102-year old Mrs Ciorstag Morrison.

Angus 'Umag' MacSween, a gentle and universally respected man, was at the helm of the *Rhum* for the final sailings; he was the last of the original 1965 crew and the only man to have served on all the Scalpay ferries.

STROME – Loch Carron (Stromeferry to North Strome)

Loch Carron thrusts into the West Highland coast between the Lochalsh and Applecross peninsulas and its precipitate, craggy southern shore follows the great fault line of the Moine Thrust. The terrain and geology west and north of this is distinctive, scenic and geologically ancient. There would be no road around the south side of Loch Carron until 1970 nor a road along its northern shore to Strome until early in the nineteenth century and, with the coming of the motor-car, the Strome ferry would be for long the only alternative to a 140-mile detour.

'This was always a beautiful journey,' wrote John Prebble sadly in 1982, a dozen years after the service had ceased, 'dark water in the shadow of the twin hills that guard the narrows, a solacing climax to the long drive from Inverness. In the 18th century the loch-shore was thickly populated, black with dry-stone cottages, green and yellow with good fields of grain. The water was famous for its shoals of herring, so plentiful, said John Knox, that they "tumbled upon the surface, and others leaped fairly out to the distance of two or three yards." His companions fired at them with lug-shot, "but we knew not with what effect." James Hogg came to Strome in 1803, on a Sunday morning in June, having travelled eleven miles over the high pass from Kintail before breakfast. He stood angrily on the southern shore, waving his hat until the ferryman came over and agreed to take him for sixpence and a dram of whisky. Sixteen years later, when Thomas Telford finished his highway along the western shore, the ferry

became the busiest in the western Highlands, linking Inverness and Dingwall with Lochalsh and the Isles. Telford's friend, Robert Southey, travelled along this new road within a few days of its completion and was delighted to discover that his carriage was the first to reach the ferry at Strome...'

Clan history here was turbulent and we know from its annals that a ferry worked the Strome narrows from at least the Middle Ages. It was probably in operation from around the fifteenth century when Strome Castle was built by the Macdonalds of Glengarry only to be demolished in 1602 by the MacKenzies of Kintail, after the female prisoners within the castle had slyly dampened the store of gunpowder.

But service through the seventeenth and eighteenth centuries seems to have been sporadic. We know that in 1803 James Hogg was directed to take the official vessel, so a ferry – or at least the recognised rights to operate one – evidently existed by that time. The hamlet by the south of the narrows has been long known as Strome Ferry and that on the north is dubbed on maps, Stromemore – though most locals simply call it North Strome.

In 1809 the Highland Roads and Bridges Commission began a new road along the north shore of Loch Carron to Achnasheen to meet the main highway to Inverness. This western highway took a decade to complete and lent new importance to the Strome ferry which was now the vital link to Plockton, Lochalsh and the Kyleakin crossing to Skye. The ferry was based on the south side and could be imperiously summoned by 'mail-horn' from the

Below left: An un-named turntable ferry dating from around 1920 was used on the Strome link until the late 1950s.

Below centre: Believed to be the *Highland Queen* of 1938, this image shows the steep and uneven nature of the early slipways.

Below right: The *Highland Queen* with a typical summer loading of tourist cars and bicycles.

Between January and March 2012, the Strome ferry was reinstated following a rock fall which blocked the road on the south side of Loch Carron. The *Glenachulish* is seen in company of the Plockton-based excursion vessel *Sula Mhor*.
(Robert Beale)

northern shore, lest there be any delay with the post.

In 1870 the new railway from Inverness made its terminus at Strome Ferry, making it for the first time an important port, with steamer-services for Portree and Stornoway and, of course, greatly increasing demand for the ferry. It remained most basic, an open craft driven by sail or oars and operating between crude jetties and it was reported that horses had to leap from pier to vessel.

The railway greatly eased the delivery of locally landed fresh fish to the distant city markets and Lewis, for instance, had then a good trade in line-caught haddock and ling, to say nothing of cured herring. The Stornoway steamer bore boxes of fish daily to Strome Ferry and the train soon rushed it south. The vessels did not, of course, sail on the Sabbath, but on occasion arrived late on a Saturday and on one weekend, to local vexation, fish-handling and train-loading continued well after midnight and into the Sabbath Day.

It was decided informally and with some emotion in the district that this must not be allowed to happen again and when, on Saturday 2nd June 1883, a laden boat did not finally berth until 23.00, over two hundred devout and angry fishermen took utter command of the pier. No work would begin or would be allowed to begin, they made plain, until after midnight the following day. When the railwaymen

nevertheless tried to access the ship and her cargo, there was considerable scuffle and emotion and they were pushed implacably back to the tracks. The stationmaster immediately telegraphed his superintendent in Inverness, who at once appealed to the police. On Sabbath morning a special train ran from Dingwall to Strome Ferry with eight sturdy officers on board, arriving at 11.00. They now stormed the pier and were repelled six times.

The protestors also declined to allow the rail men to start the steam-engines for their cranes at 22.30. Then at midnight, the mass of fishermen advanced menacingly on the station but only to check the time. Being satisfied it was now midnight, they were happy to disperse and the day-old cargo could at last be transferred.

There was some unease and protest the next weekend too, but on Sabbath 19th June there was no demonstration of any sort. The shunned railway men were left to defile the day as they pleased. Local ministers had evidently been at work, quietly convincing the good fishermen that – whatever the legalities – protest, menaces and any sort of violence broke the Sabbath as much as unnecessary work.

We know that

The **Strome Castle** (II) dated from 1959 and is seen on passage across Loch Carron. Following the route's closure just eleven years later, both she and the earlier **Pride of Strome** were simply abandoned on the north shore of the loch.

for some years in the nineteenth century a Christopher Finlayson held the ferry-rights and his descendants still live in Lochcarron and district. In the first decade of the twentieth century improvements were made to the ferry and cars were certainly being carried across Loch Carron by the First World War. But there were still very few cars about in those days and, by that time the railway ran all the way to Kyle of Lochalsh, which had been reached in 1897. The Strome ferry was really only of importance to those who lived north of the loch and west of Lochcarron village.

The odd vehicle was loaded (with the help of planks) onto a broad-beamed barge, which was probably towed across in calm conditions. The Strome passage is much easier than others as unlike Kylerhea, there are no reefs or rocks to worry about and there is no great tide-race but the loch is very exposed to westerly gales (and the backwash and swell from northerly ones). It is also rather vulnerable to seiches - a thermal phenomenon that can cause a very fast rise in the water level and with unexpected currents.

The first turntable ferry on the route was introduced in the years following the Great War. It was a motorised timber-hulled vessel capable of carrying one bus or two small cars and was probably based on

the *Glencoe* of 1912 which was operating down at Ballachulish. In 1929 the fare to cross with a vehicle was 10 shillings (50p), the same as it was at Dornie. Though her name – if she bore one – cannot be confirmed, one very old resident thinks she may have been the *Maid of Strome*.

But Strome service, this crude one-car ferry, with probably the odd rowing boat in assistance was grossly inadequate and would remain so for many years to come. This in part was a consequence of serious railway competition for the carriage of cars (most, then driven by sporting gentry.) From practically the start of service to Kyle of Lochalsh, freight of motor cars was offered using special wagon trains from Kyle, Strome Ferry or Strathcarron. In fact, it was cheaper - just seven shillings or 35p for carriage by rail, but ten shillings (50p) for the epic freight of your roadster over Loch Carron. The only nuisance was the Company's requirement of two days' notice.

By the 1950s the train ran three times a day in each direction between Kyle of Lochalsh and Strathcarron with an intermediate stop at Strome. Cars were still conveyed, but now it cost twice as much as passage by the ferry. The price though, was more than double that of the marine alternative. In 1953 for instance, the

Below left: As the *Highland Queen* or *Strome Castle* (I) plods across Loch Carron carrying two cars, the queue grows longer. Larger ferries eventually helped to ease the problem to some extent but the opening of the new by-pass on the southern shore brought about the service's premature closure.

Below right: The splendid *Pride of Strome* is seen discharging her vehicles at South Strome.

ferry cost 10 shillings (50p) for a car whilst the railway cost 23 shillings (£1.15) for a car under 15hp from Kyle or 18 shillings (80p) from Strome to Strathcarron. It was also much more inconvenient as a car for the 06.25 from Kyle had to be loaded by 18.00 the previous day and also with an empty petrol tank.

The ferry service was never really run properly or granted adequate investment. In 1937 Sir William Anstruther-Gray, the Tory Member for North Lanarkshire, was with his stately car stuck aboard the craft for three hours when low tide prevented the ferry from unloading – a tale he pointedly related in Parliament after the state of the tide did not allow the vessel to unload. It would take two decades more before better slipways were built and even then, at extreme low tide, the service could be briefly suspended.

By the late 1930s, as many as eighty cars daily could seek passage and, with a craft able only to convey one at a time, motorists could wait up to three hours for passage. A young local man, George Cumming, now acquired the Strome ferry rights with the help and funding of his family. Cumming would later also own the North Strome Inn, the pub adjacent to the Stromemore slipway, and is well remembered in the district as a colourful character.

He was eager to improve the service and rapidly ordered a larger boat. The new, 2-car *Highland Queen* arrived in August 1938 and the neat, timber-hulled vessel was more powerful and more sophisticated than her prosaic predecessor. That veteran was no

doubt retained for some time for relief and back-up, but hard facts are hard to come by for most of the service's history. We know that a second 2-car turntable ferry, *Strome Castle* (I) was introduced some years later – probably during the war.

Timetables for 1953 show that ferry operated continuously from 08.00 until 21.00 during summer, and 09.00 until 17.00 in winter. There would have been frequent delays at low tide until the new slipways were completed. There was no Sunday service – and never would be – but traffic through the fifties continued implacably to increase. In high summer the long queues and, on occasion, even overnight wait for a crossing became increasingly scandalous.

As early as 1955 there were calls for a bridge over the straits or a bypass road by some route along the south side to Strathcarron, or at the very least for the ferry service to be wrested from Cumming's hands by the County Council.

In 1958 the Royal Automobile Club contacted Ross and Cromarty Highways Committee about the number of complaints they had received regarding the ferry at Stromeferry. In future guidebooks they would advise their members to avoid the ferry unless drastic improvements were made. Confronted and in a remarkable exchange Messrs R and G Cummings gave assurances that they would consider introducing more car ferries and not stopping for a lunch break. It was also noted that the Cummings family were suspending the service at night at 17.00 when, only

three years earlier, in 1955 they had agreed with the council to operate until 21.00.

In 1958 over 20,000 vehicles were carried and the ageing little boats now seriously struggled. Larger tonnage was needed and under political pressure, the Cummings laid an order with James Noble (Boatbuilders) Ltd of Fraserburgh. Meanwhile, the council spent £30,000 rebuilding high, long, new and rather splendid slipways in preparation for the new, larger vessels. The modified slips allowed operations at all states of the tide and, steel-trimmed, of delicate curve and with a neat slotted rail down the centre for ready warping (by a hooked line) as the ferry took the pier, still impress today. But this was, after all a private enterprise. The scale of such generosity from the public purse raised many eyebrows and may well have accelerated the final approval of the bypass.

The new *Strome Castle* (II) was very similar in lines and design to the later Ballachulish craft, could carry six cars and was introduced for the summer of 1959. But so remorselessly was motor-tourism growing that her impact was minimal. 'Although Strome Ferry, across Loch Carron now has a six-car boat in addition to two two-car boats,' murmured the 'Glasgow Herald' on 7th August, 'delays of three hours, and on occasion, five hours, occur.'

It was no better the following year and, in June 1960, the Ross and Cromarty MP – a Unionist member, Sir John MacLeod – tabled a written question to the Secretary of State for Scotland, John McLay. Was his Honourable Friend aware 'that recently members of the public had to wait in a queue of forty-two cars for three hours before getting across Strome Ferry; and what action did he propose to take to provide a by-pass road?

Considering that Sir John sat on the Government side, later discussion – on the 28th June - in the chamber was distinctly robust.

'My Right Honourable Friend is aware that from time to time there are delays at Strome Ferry,' insisted Dumfriesshire MP Niall Macpherson, deputising for McLay, 'but I am unable to say when a bypass, which would cost over half a million pounds, can be fitted into the road programme.'

'Is the Joint Under-Secretary unaware that this is an absolute scandal?' snapped Sir John, to cheerful cries

of 'Hear! Hear!' 'It is totally against this Government's policy of encouraging tourism in the Highlands, and all authoritative bodies believe that this road should bypass Strome Ferry as soon as possible.'

'As my Honourable Friend knows – and he has been to see my Right Honourable Friend about this – there has been a considerable improvement in that a six-car ferryboat was introduced last year,' argued MacPherson. 'We have not had a whole year to see how that will work, but towards the end of the tourist season my Right Honourable Friend will be glad to discuss the matter with my Honourable Friend.'

'This is when the six-car ferry is in operation,' said Sir John darkly, 'and it is only the beginning of the season.'

'It would be quite wrong to give the impression that the degree of waiting to which my Honourable Friend has referred is anything like a regular occurrence; it certainly is not. While there are delays, it is only at the peak periods that there are delays of an hour or more.'

Such was the position of a vital Highland highway – the most convenient route for many in Wester Ross to reach their county capital of Dingwall, or for anyone north of Lochcarron to get to Skye or Lochaber, or for anyone from the south to explore the charms of the

The *Strome Castle* (II) is seen at South Strome. The vessels were always maintained in a beautiful condition and if there was ever a case for a seasonal ferry revival, then surely this is a route worth re-evaluating.
(AE Glen/Bruce Peter)

The *Pride of Strome* served for only eight years before the service was closed. Her hulk lies abandoned on the north shore of Loch Carron. *(Brian Maxted)*

Applecross peninsula. Unlike Ballachulish, there was no half-hour spin round the loch as an alternative nor, unlike those anxious to avoid Kyleakin, could they simply take an alternative ferry.

Soon afterwards, as if to appease Sir John MacLeod, the Cummings ordered an additional vessel – not, though, from Noble's, but from J and G Forbes Co. (Boatbuilders) Ltd of Sandhaven, also on the Buchan coast. The result was one of the best and most interesting turntable ferries ever built and the only one ever constructed by this company. Sadly she would have a pitiably short career.

The oak-hulled, twin-screw and powerful *Pride of Strome* was in service for the summer of 1962, of pleasing appearance and significantly bigger than the *Strome Castle* (II), able to squeeze on eight or nine cars. She was of noticeably higher freeboard and can be distinguished in photographs by her diagonal timber strapping – most wooden turntable ferries had horizontal belting; her fully enclosed wheelhouse and the tripod mainmast atop. Her arrival saw the last of the old 2-car ferries quit the stage. The *Highland Queen* seems simply to have been abandoned on the beach some yards west of the southern, Strome Ferry slip – probably after the commissioning of *Strome Castle* (II) and a keel can still be seen. The first *Strome Castle* was, on the advent of the *Pride of* Strome, sold for use as a dive-support vessel. She lost her turntable, acquired her cabin, and was finally left to rot as she chose on the shingle side of the northern, Stromemore slipway.

But management issues apart, Strome – like Kyleakin – was fast proving a situation where turntable ferries were no longer up to the job, at least with the

summer traffic offering by the mid 1960s and with only one loading-berth on either side. The queues became ever more prodigious – a 6-hour wait to cross on a steamy August day, was by no means uncommon while the queue for passage on the southern side, often stretched back to Achmore. On a good day and toiling as best they could, the ferrymen could convey just under a thousand cars. In a West Highland guidebook written just before the decade's end, W H Murray bluntly declared that the service had been 'long since overwhelmed.' Had corner-loading ferries on the scale of the *Rosehaugh* or the *Maid of Glencoul* materialised, it might have been different but for such vessels George Cumming had not the vision or the funds.

The issue may even have ended Sir John MacLeod's career; in October 1964 he lost Ross and Cromarty to a young Skye-reared teacher, Russell Johnstone. The new Liberal member had to wait but a year for final approval, in October 1965, of a Strome by-pass.

George Cumming had fought the idea, and proposals for a bridge tooth and nail and he had excellent lawyers who knew the fine details of ferry rights. The authorities had rapidly ascertained the straits could not lawfully be spanned against his wishes nor, it seems, were they able to buy him out. Shrewd steps had been taken to secure his interests, as the 'Ross-shire Journal' announced in the small print – on 23rd April that year:

Among companies registered in Scotland were: (1) Strome Ferry Service Ltd, to operate the Strome Ferry Service at Loch Carron. Capital: £10,000 in £1 shares. Directors: Robert J Cumming, Banff; and George S M Cumming, North Strome, Strome Ferry. (2) Strome Ferry (Properties) Ltd, to acquire ferry rights between North Strome and South Strome. Capital: £50,000 in £1 shares. Directors as (1.)

But the Cummings could not stop the road, which advanced remorselessly over the mountainside and, to the unease of many locals, beneath a long length of precipitous, rotten rock by the shore at Attadale, parallel to the railway. The Council had been unable to buy the necessary land for passage through that estate's grounds and did not seek a compulsory-purchase order. It is probable, besides, for the Beeching axe had just fallen and railway routes were vanishing all over the country that it was calculated the Kyle line would soon be history, and the road could then readily be widened. For now a concrete avalanche shelter was prudently built, for both trains and cars at a particularly tight spot.

The new, narrow, winding 7-mile highway duly opened in October 1970, a year later than at first forecast. It proved from the start vulnerable to ice and snow and, worse, to rock falls. The A890 has been repeatedly closed. On one occasion a mini-bus laden with local teenagers was fortunate to avoid a serious accident as boulders rained down all around them. Some in Lochcarron village genuinely fear that a truly enormous landslide could trigger a tsunami and inundate the township itself. And they had immediately lost their ferry.

'It was my hope to put my car on the last boat to make the crossing,' John Prebble recalled, 'but, when I arrived, coming through the pass at Achnashellach to a wondrous sunset, I found the eastern road already open and the ferry-boat moored and idle. Later that year, when I came again, the boat was gone, and the only movement offshore was a lone shag, straight-necked and black above the water, direct in flight and hurrying seaward to its evening rest on a rock-island beyond the narrows.'

George Cumming's decision simply to cease operation as soon as the new road opened still baffles, and remains the stuff of conspiracy theories in the community. A continued Strome ferry would have retained Lochcarron in the main tourist highway, been a more convenient way to Lochalsh for many locals – especially west of the village, the journey south from Ardaneaskan now requiring an entire circuit of the loch – and generally benefitted the Applecross peninsula. A summer-only operation would be perfectly viable even now. But the ferries just stopped. 'Everybody I know up there,' remarked one son of Lochcarron in February 2012, 'reckoned the bypass would have lost its appeal after the first few months if they were still running. Nobody could understand why George Cumming stopped the service and wouldn't sell the ferries or the ferry rights'.

What is certain is that these splendid and really rather new boats were simply tied up at moorings in a bay east of Stromemore, and abandoned by their owner. Over the years they pitiably deteriorated.

They were besides mercilessly looted and vandalised, bits taken, wheelhouse windows smashed. The *Strome Castle* (II) broke her rotted cables, fetched up on the shore, and by the decade's end was flooding. Each time the tide rose and fell, she would fill up and empty. By the mid 1980s, she had been washed up the loch by storm. The hulk survives, but has been moved at least once more since by the elements. The *Pride of Strome* – still only eight years old – suffered no less horror. On one occasion that particularly shocked the community, some unknown lout or louts got aboard, lowered both ramps, and then did their best to demolish her wheelhouse by swinging the vehicle-deck round and round, back and fore, bash upon bash. Then her mooring-chains were stolen and she too ended up, at length broken-backed, on the beach. The remains of both vessels can be visited still.

And then, over forty years after their demise, there was an astonishingly remarkable turn of events.

Shortly before Christmas 2011, a massive rock fall closed the A890 at Attadale and although quickly cleared, it was fast ascertained that the cliff face was in far too dangerous and cracked a condition to allow traffic on the highway for weeks to come. Almost a decade earlier, Highland Council had prudently put the Kylerhea ferry *Glenachulish* on brief trial of both Strome slips, for their contingency-planning, and now she was immediately offered by her directors for emergency assistance. The 1969 vessel was conveniently to hand, too; Kishorn, just to the north of Lochcarron, is her usual winter's rest. Though negotiations were brisk and her directors were very eager to help, in an age obsessed with health and safety and with the additional complication of the seasonal holiday it was mid-January before everything was in order. For one, the Cumming family still held the rights, and had to be contacted for permission and there was much else to repair and to organise.

But on Friday 13th January and again the following day, the *Glenachulish* put in practice at the Strome slips and from late on the morning of Monday 16th service resumed almost as if it had never gone. One village elder, looking on, breathed, 'I never thought I'd see a turntable ferry at Strome again.' Skippers from the old days, tottered out to have a look, to meet her crew and be generous with their memories and still more with their advice.

Concerned that the small 6-car ferry might be swamped with traffic, the Highland Council continued to display signs from either end declaring the A890 to be closed by Loch Carron and directing a detour by Invermoriston, stressed that the service was primarily for local residents; gave the service minimal publicity and indeed drove quite a hard bargain for her hire. She herself had but the vulnerability of a single engine and, though of similar dimensions to the last *Strome Castle*, was sailing a generation later in an age of bigger cars. And the weight-limit – nine metric tonnes - precluded the biggest trucks, although on Friday 27th January she was able to convey several heavy lorries and a hefty digger – one at a time - chocks being laid under her ramps as they loaded and sterling-board over her planks.

Passage was free but tickets had to be collected from marshals before approaching the piers. On the north side, this was by particularly inconvenient arrangement, as one had to drive out east of Lochcarron village to the local golf course and back again. This reflected the very limited parking and marshalling area at North Strome. On the south side, one simply accepted a ticket from the booth at the stop of the steep road down to station and slip and handed it solemnly over on boarding. A locally owned summer cruise-vessel the *Sula Mhor* made passenger sailings over the narrows, primarily for pupils attending Plockton High School and settled on a timetable from 08.00 to 18.00 daily. In the first week of service, the *Glenachulish* sailed from 09.00 to 17.00, which was of no help to most commuting to work in Lochalsh. There was no Sunday car ferry service but the *Sula Mhor* sailed to a skeletal timetable. There was in fact little demand from pedestrians as, for most the train (which continued to run) was almost as convenient.

The usual skippers and crew from Kylerhea were employed, in two crews, changing around 13.00. The Highland Council spent considerable sums and went to great trouble to ensure the smoothest arrangements. Both slipways were given quick repairs, mooring-rings replaced and safety-railings added above the berthing area. Temporary flood lighting was provided on both sides – with noisy generators – and everywhere, either side of the passage, seethed with genial council employees in yellow jackets and chattering 2-way radios. The crew, working as hard as they were in cold and often very unpleasant conditions, were all but inundated with home baking.

After first trials on Friday 13th January, she commenced a near ten-week stint from 16th until Friday 23rd March 2012, during which time she carried over 7,800 cars, the vessel saving motorists a 140 mile-detour via Inverness. On several days storms prevented operation; she was off for a few for MCA checks and repair after an unfortunate grounding on Thursday 2nd March (an unexpected seiche pushed her out from the North Strome slip on first approach, and on her second her engine stalled at a critical moment) and she lost another day after more mechanical problems. She had not yet had her annual overhaul, and the unwonted swell of Loch Carron, it emerged, had stirred up a lot of old 'gunk' in her fuel tank. Her skippers were puzzled by February's end, to note that their command was sitting significantly lower in the water. Then they remembered that there had been a week or two of sustained heavy rain affecting the salinity of Loch Carron, and hence the Kylerhea ferry's buoyancy. Thus the little ship maintained, for over two months and with remarkable success, a lifeline service and maintained it with honour.

Meanwhile specialist engineers seethed over the Attadale rock face; there was soon not a room to be had for the night in the parish and from mid March rubber matting was laid on the railway to allow vehicles to drive along the tracks when no train was due. On this 'Scalectrix Road', as it was cheerfully dubbed by locals, the A890 was opened to vehicles, under careful supervision, on 24th March, as the *Glenachulish* had now urgently to go for overhaul to be ready for her Kylerhea duties by 1st May. The Strome bypass was fully cleared for traffic on 23rd April but closed briefly, eight months later at Christmas, by another rock fall. All agree that a permanent solution is urgently needed, but in hard economic times and continued public austerity a re-routed road, a bridge, or even a restored permanent ferry seem unlikely in the near future.

THE DEVELOPMENT OF THE TURNTABLE FERRY

The design of the turntable ferry is worth consideration. Many factors went into the design of these boats. They worked narrow sea-lochs or island straits and in these close confines and strong tides, they had to contend with formidable currents. The boats had to be fully capable in these conditions. They had also to be stable enough to carry vehicles and this entailed a broad beam. The wider any vessel is in relation to her length, the more resistance her hull offers and the slower she is. Early boats had sharp bows to slice through the water but, as the ferries became wider - taking more cars - the limit was reached as to how narrow the bow could be.

Before the turntable vessels arrived at the crossings, there were rowing boats designed to take foot passengers and a few horses or a cart in operation. Stability was paramount in the turbulent waters so the vessels were made wider and beamier to increase the load and the safety of those on board. In order to have the power to move these boats, the oars, or sweeps, were extremely long and it was not unknown for the passengers to be asked to help row themselves!

The arrival of the motor car was a challenge to these ferrymen and in the early days cars were loaded on to large barges by means of two wooden planks and then secured to the vessel, tied through the wheel spokes as it was rowed across. On the Kyleakin

The Maid of Kylesku at her southern slipway.

Below: With the glorious backdrop of the North West Highlands, *The Maid of Kylesku* creeps up to the slipway at Unapool.

Bottom right: This view of the *Queen of Kylesku* gives a good impression of her deck space, bridge and passenger lounge.

crossing it is known that a car-carrying barge was often towed across by a small motor launch from 1914, but the first car was carried across Loch Leven at Ballachulish in 1906 and, six years later, the *Glencoe* – the first turntable ferry anywhere was placed in service. It was a rather crude vessel with a basic turntable which allowed loading at most states of the tide from a gradually graded slipway. But the principle was ingenious and it is a pity we do not know who came up with it.

At normal levels the boat would simply berth alongside the slip and rotate its turntable to line the ramp up with the slip. Once unloaded and loaded up again the turntable would be spun round 180 degrees so the cars were facing the right way for disembarkation.

At extremely low tides some vessels did what became known as a 'T bone' landing. This was when the boat came alongside the end of the slipway and unloaded at right angles to the end of the slip, thus creating a T shape. And the first, nameless turntable ferry at Kylesku was able to end load on at least one of the slips.

On the Corran crossing another way of unloading was to come alongside the end of the old Nether Lochaber slip bow-out at very low tides, and have the

turntable unloading stern first, with the cars disembarking near the wheelhouse rather than the bow.

As roads became busier so larger ferries were needed. The early turntables mainly catered for one standard sized car but by the late 1930s, two-car vessels were appearing.

The first four-car ferries came in the early 1950s and from the late 1950s six-car ferries were being introduced. It was not uncommon to aid stability when loading by making the first vehicle drive on and sit in the centre of the turntable, until the following car had loaded.

The culmination of the turntable design was the 1973 *Lochaber* which was built for use at Corran and could accommodate nine large cars. Fully laden her great vehicle-deck proved really beyond manual operation and hydraulic machinery had to be added, the turntable ferry had reached its physical and practical limits.

As ferries became larger they also needed to become more manoeuvrable. The first vessel with twin engines was the *Portree* (l) of 1951 and all subsequent Kyleakin vessels had twin screws. Apart from greater power, boats with two propellers respond much better to the helm and there is particular advantage when going astern. But a twin-screw craft has generally a deeper draught. Besides, they have much stronger 'updraught', apt to suck up a boil of silt, sand, gravel and seaweed where there is little depth of water. In such conditions there is also the risk of cavitation, when the churning screws can create physical vacuums as they spin, causing stresses that can tear chunks out of the propellers themselves.

This meant that not many other routes utilized boats with twin engines as they operated alongside shallower slipways. Ballachulish, for example had no twin-screw vessels and it is not thought that one could work Kylerhea. Strome on the other hand benefited from one twin-screw vessel, named *Pride of Strome*, which was the last vessel built for use there and was a culmination of lessons learnt with the previous vessels on the route. With her twin engines she was therefore much easier to handle than the similar *Strome Castle* (II) built only three years earlier.

Most of the ferries were wooden. The 1942 *Cuillin* on the Kyleakin route was the first steel-hulled turntable vessel. This did not become standard across the whole turntable network as later vessels such as the *Pride of Strome* and *Lochaber* were still built of timber. Steel did, however, become the material of choice at Kyleakin.

Early ramps were primitive; little more than broad planks kept in place when stowed by hooked chains and lowered by hand when needed. As ramps became larger and heavier and had to take larger loads, they were soon made from metal and to aid the ferrymen, and a counter-weighted system was developed. Aluminium ramps, lighter and safer, became standard at Ballachulish from the commissioning of the *Glen Mallie* in 1959. The 1964 *Gleann Mhor* was the first vessel to have spring-braced ramps – safer in operation - and later vessels followed suit.

Wheelhouses for the skipper were also a late addition to the turntable ferries. The first vessel with sheltered steering was the 1951 *Portree* (I) built for service on the Kyleakin crossing; she took up service the following year and was also the first turntable ferry with a passenger saloon. All subsequent vessels were equipped with a wheelhouse except for *The Maid of Kylesku*, whose crew braved the elements to the last, and the 1955-built *Appin Chief* (which was later given one). The *Maid of Luing*, built in 1953 for service on the Cuan Sound, was unique amongst turntable vessels in that her wheelhouse was situated at the bow of the boat. Covered passenger accommodation, though, was provided only at Kyleakin (from 1951), Kessock, Corran (from 1959, with the *Ben Keil* and her successors) and Kylesku (with the arrival of the *Queen*

A Bedford OB coach is swung on the deck of the **Highland Queen** at Strome. *(Robert Grieves collection)*

of Kylesku in 1967.) Elsewhere, foot-passengers had to stand on the open vehicle-deck and endure the weather as they could. The *Inbhir-Nis* on the Kessock crossing from 1953 was also unique in that the passenger accommodation had its own ramp lowered onto the slip, to keep pedestrians clear of the turntable and ramps.

In short, three basic designs of turntable developed.

The 1st generation turntable ferries were crude affairs. Conveying between one and two cars they were shaped like a traditionally built heavy-duty motor boat with a turntable placed on board. They were steered from an open steering position at the stern of the vessel. Ramps were made of wood and were manually operated. These boats were built between 1912 and 1940.

The 2nd generation turntable ferries usually carried between two and four vehicles. The hull shape was different from the earlier vessels, being more barge shaped, with a turntable placed on board. The first steel hulled vessel falls into this category. The ramps changed from wooden to steel and were designed to use a counter-weight system. The vessel was still steered from an open position at the stern. These were built between 1935 and 1955.

Finally **the 3rd generation** turntable ferry was introduced from 1951 and the last was built in 1973. These vessels had wheelhouses and carried between four and nine vehicles. They had metal ramps which were operated with a counter-weight system, or from

The *Glen Mallie* is seen
crossing the Ballachulish
Narrows when new.
(GL Watson Ltd 2012)

1959 a spring loaded system. Some of these vessels had twin engines and twin screws and were highly manoeuvrable, but the choice of material was still dependant on the route and wood was used, as well as steel.

Apart from one route, all the turntable ferries in Scotland operated on the west coast but many of the boats were built along a short stretch of the east coast. Banff delivered a few boats in the 1930s from Messrs Stevenson & Asher Boat builders and Forbes of Sandhaven provided one of the best equipped, the *Pride of Strome*.

However, one name stands out from the fleet list, that of James Noble (Boatbuilders) Ltd of Fraserburgh. Though kept in brisk trade for their fine fishing-boats, in the 1950s and 1960s they built a succession of turntable ferries for Ballachulish, Bonawe, Corran, Cuan, Kessock, Kylesku and Strome. Several enjoyed second careers (or at least relief) at Kyleakin and Scalpay.

The Kyle of Lochalsh-Kyleakin route was a disconnected limb of the Clyde based Caledonian Steam Packet Co. Ltd and their loyalty shows. Apart from the *Kyleakin* (I), from Goole, all their turntable and side loading vessels were built within the confines of the Clyde. They first went to Hugh McLean and Sons Ltd of Renfrew for the *Moil* and then commissioned five vessels from William Denny and Bros Ltd of Dumbarton. The Ailsa Shipbuilding Co. Ltd of Troon provided two turntables and a side-loader whilst James Lamont and Company Ltd, Port Glasgow built the two remaining side-loaders.

By the mid 1960s, however, the limitations of the design were evident and only two more turntable ferries would be built. They could not handle a heavy volume of car traffic and that became embarrassingly obvious in high summer, at Strome (where there was no convenient road alternative) and at Kyleakin, even with four craft shuttling at once and with three loading-berths at Kyle and two at Kyleakin. And, as road-haulage rapidly became the norm, they could not convey lorries much heavier than nine metric tons.

Some of the vessels went on to have careers as work barges after their public working lives were over; other discarded craft were simply beached near their old run. Today, then, we enjoy only one working example of a turntable ferry, the *Glenachulish*, which every year between Easter and October provides stalwart service between Glenelg and Kylerhea.

FLEET LIST

Where a ferry was replaced by a ship of the same name, the number of the vessel appears in brackets, ie, *Scalpay* (II) was the second vessel to be named *Scalpay*. If the number appears outside brackets as in *Lochalsh II*, then the 'II' was part of the registered name. Confusingly, especially at Kyleakin, vessels often were renamed to allow their name to be used by a new vessel. For example the (1951) *Lochalsh* (I) was renamed *Lochalsh II* (I) to make way for the (1957) *Lochalsh* (II) to use the name. Then 14 years later we see the (1957) *Lochalsh* (II) being renamed *Lochalsh II* (II) to make the name available for the (1971) *Lochalsh* (III). This is one reason why keeping track of these vessels can be difficult at times.

If a vessel served at more than one location, to avoid repetition the fate of that vessel will be in the notes section in the table for the final route it served on. For clarity, on routes where not every vessel was a turntable ferry, non-turntable vehicle carrying vessels are listed but marked with **. Purely passenger ferries are generally not listed.

BALLACHULISH

Name	Built Acquired Disposed of Broken up	Cars (of average size) Hull type	Engine/ propulsion	Builder	Notes
Glencoe (I)	1912 1912 1935 1936	1 Wood	1 x 15-20 hp Kelvin. Single screw.	McGruer & Company, Clynder, Gareloch	First turntable ferry built. Probably displaced upon arrival of *Maid of Glencoe* (I). May have made a trip to Ardgour. Sold for use at Corran. Wrecked in a storm in late 1936.
Glencoe (II)	1926 1926 1936 C1938	1 Wood	1 x Kelvin engine. Single screw.	Unknown	Remained in service until displaced by *Queen of Glen Albyn*. Sold to Corran and replaced by the *North Argyll*.
Maid of Glencoe (I)	1935 1935 1955 C1956	2 Wood	1 x 36 hp Gleniffer. Single screw.	Hugh MacLean & Sons Ltd, Renfrew	Displaced by the *Appin Chief*. Broken up and used for spares for the other Ballachulish vessels in 1956.
Queen of Glen Albyn	1936 1936 1959 C1964	2 Wood	1 x 36 hp Gleniffer. Re-engined June 1949 with 1 x 4 cylinder Gleniffer diesel. Single screw.	Messrs Stevenson & Asher Boat builders, Banff	Displaced by the arrival of *Maid of Glencoe* (II). Sold on for use at Glenelg.
Mamore	1951 1951 1959 C1967	4 Wood	1 x 4 cylinder Gleniffer diesel. Single screw.	James Noble (Fraserburgh) Ltd	As built she was steered from an exposed position at the stern. Received a basic shelter after a subsequent refit. Displaced by the *Glen Mallie* in 1959 and sold to Sutherland County Council for £1,200 who used her as a relief vessel on the crossing at Kylesku.
Appin Chief	1955 1955 1961 C1975	4 Wood	1 x 4 cylinder Gleniffer diesel. Re-engined late 1958 with another Gleniffer. Single screw.	James Noble (Fraserburgh) Ltd	Sold on for further service at Glenelg. Gained a wheelhouse before 1958, probably soon after the *Maid of Glencoe* (II) arrived in 1957. Also served at Scalpay on relief in 1968 and 1969.

Maid of Glencoe (II)	1956 1957 1965 1971	4 Wood	1 x 4 cylinder Gleniffer. Re-engined late 1958 with 1 x Kelvin, replaced later by 1 x 4 cylinder Gleniffer. Single screw.	James Noble (Fraserburgh) Ltd	Displaced from Ballchulish by the *Glen Loy*. Sold to David MacBrayne and renamed *Scalpay* (I) for service at Scalpay.
Glen Mallie	1959 1959 1969 C1985	6 Wood	1 x Gleniffer 4 cylinder diesel. Single screw.	James Noble (Fraserburgh) Ltd	Sold for use at Glenelg in 1969. Also served in relief capacity at Cuan in 1978, Scalpay in 1971, '72, '73, '74 and '75, as well as Kyle of Lochalsh in 1971 and '72.
Glen Duror	1961 1961 1975 C1977	6 Wood	1 x Gleniffer 4 cylinder diesel. Single screw.	James Noble (Fraserburgh) Ltd	Displaced upon opening of Ballachulish bridge. Sold for £3,000 to a local contractor who used her as a works barge on the Caledonian Canal at Muirtown in 1976 and 1977. Abandoned on the shores of Loch Lochy.
Glen Loy	1964 1964 1975 C1980	6 Wood	1 x Gleniffer 4 cylinder diesel. Single screw.	James Noble (Fraserburgh) Ltd	Displaced upon opening of Ballachulish bridge. Sold to UEG Trials Ltd for £4,500. They probably used her for a pontoon in relation to their dive school at Fort William. She was seen moored in 1977 in reasonable condition and was eventually abandoned at Trislaig, opposite Fort William.
Glenachulish	1969 1969 1975 Still operational	6 Steel	180 hp Kelvin T6. Single screw.	Ailsa Shipbuilding Company, Troon	Displaced upon opening of Ballachulish bridge. Acquired by Highland Regional Council. Served as relief vessel at Corran, Kessock and Kylesku between 1975 and 1982 before being sold in 1983 for service at Glenelg. Also served at Strome in 2012.

There is a possibility there was another single vehicle ferry introduced around the time of the first *Glencoe* (I) but this has not been confirmed. Various rowing boats and motor launches were used for passenger only service including the *Babe, Corsair, Mila* and *Malus*.

BONAWE

Name	Built Acquired Disposed of Broken up	Cars (of average size) Hull type	Engine/ propulsion	Builder	Notes
Deirdre	1936 1937 1940 C1946	4 Wood	Single screw.	Hugh MacLean & Sons Ltd, Renfrew	Operated until outbreak of WW2. During WW2 she worked in Orkney helping with cement and concrete works for the Churchill Barrier submarine defences. Returned to Bonawe, beached in the West Harbour and eventually burned where she lay.
Dhuirnish	1956 1956 1967 C1988	4 Wood (6 when converted to bow-loading operation)	2 x 4 cylinder Gleniffer. Twin screw.	James Noble (Fraserburgh) Ltd	Ferry ceased in 1967 but was sold in late 1966 to Bute Ferry Co who converted her to bow loading for use at Colintraive, capacity was increased to 6 and she operated there between 1967 – 1971. Sold to Robert Beattie of Rothesay for £900 for use as rival ferry between Port Bannatyne and Ardyne in 1971 but service failed after 2 weeks. Noted as barge at Kerrera in late 1970s. In use at Inchmarnock in October 1985. Beached on Inchmarnock.

CORRAN

Name	Built Acquired Disposed of Broken up	Cars (of average size) Hull type	Engine/ propulsion	Builder	Notes
Un-named	191X 1934 C1935 C1935	1 Wood	1 x Kelvin petrol/paraffin engine. Single screw.	Unknown	First motor ferry at Corran. She was a converted lifeboat and was nearly 20 years old when purchased. Probably laid up after 'The White Boat' entered service later in 1935.
Un-named vessel known as 'The White Boat'. Previously the Glencoe (I).	1912 1935 1936 1936	1 Wood	1 x 15-20 hp Kelvin. Single screw.	McGruer & Company, Clynder, Gareloch	Purchased from Ballachulish where she was the Glencoe (I). She replaced the ex lifeboat and, following a complete refit, was lost in a storm in December 1936.
Un-named vessel known as 'The Grey Boat'and later 'Tough' ex Glencoe (II).	1926 1936 1937 1937	1 Wood	1 x Kelvin engine. Single screw.	Unknown	Chartered when 'The White Boat' was out of service due to a breakdown and then purchased so that a reliable service could be operated for the summer of 1936. She remained in service until the North Argyll had settled in. She was the ex Ballachulish vessel Glencoe (II).
North Argyll	1937 1937 1946 1946	1 Wood	1 x 4 cylinder 30 hp Kelvin replaced later by a 2 cylinder Kelvin. Single screw.	John Henderson & Sons Boat Builders of Mallaig	Built of wood she was a 1 car vessel which utilised the turntable of the 'Tough'. She operated until replaced by the Maid of Glengour and was laid aside on the beach.
Maid of Glengour	1946 1946 C1952 C1955	2 Wood	1 x 4 cylinder 30 hp Kelvin, from the North Argyll. Single screw.	James Noble (Fraserburgh) Ltd	Built as a replacement for the North Argyll. She served until the Garven had settled in and was sold to a local owner.
Garven	1949 1949 1964 C1970	4 Wood	Single screw. Wheelhouse added 1951/52	James Noble (Fraserburgh) Ltd	Served at Corran most likely until the introduction of the Gleann Mhor in 1964. Received a wheelhouse later in career. She was sold to Wiggins Teape and used as a tender at Corpach Pulp Mill after the Gleann Mhor was introduced.
Ben Keil	1959 1959 1973 C1977	6 Wood	Twin screw.	James Noble (Fraserburgh) Ltd	Displaced from Corran by the Lochaber. Believed scrapped at Crinan.
Gleann Mhor	1964 1964 1982 C1985	6 comfortably managed, 9 small ones at a squeeze) Wood	Twin screw.	James Noble (Fraserburgh) Ltd	Made redundant by the arrival of the Rosehaugh. Used as a barge at Ulva between C1982 and C1985 and abandoned there. First ferry with spring loaded ramps.
Lochaber	1973 1973 1985 C1996	9 Wood	Twin screw.	James Noble (Fraserburgh) Ltd	Displaced by Maid of Glencoul in 1984 and laid up at Ardgour until 1985. Sold to Marine Harvest Ltd of Loch Sunart for use servicing fish farms. Irreparably damaged in storm in 1996 when ripped from moorings.
Rosehaugh	1967 1982 2001 Still operational	14 Steel	Voith Schneider units.	Berwick Shipyard	Came to Corran in 1982 after being displaced by a bridge from Kessock. Displaced from Corran in 2001 MacDonald Ferries, operating from Invergordon supplying oil rigs.

| **Maid of Glencoul** | 1975 1984 Still operational at Corran | 18 Steel | Twin Caterpillar diesel 2 x M6cy 500bhp. Voith Schneider units. | MacCrindle Shipbuilding Ltd, Ardrossan | Displaced from Kylesku in 1984 after opening of bridge. Arrived at Corran and was main vessel until 2001. The arrival of the *Corran* now means she is the spare vessel. |
| **Corran** | 2001 2001 Still operational at Corran | 30 Steel | Cummins V12 38L engines, Replaced in 2008 with Cummins KTA 19 19L engines. 2 x Voith propulsion units. Type 16 K.G. | George Prior Engineering (Yorkshire) Ltd, Hull | First purpose built ferry for Corran since the *Lochaber* of 1974. She provides the main service with *Maid of Glencoul* in reserve. |

The *Glenachulish* also served here occasionally on relief between 1975 and 1982. The *Scalpay* (II) covered for the *Gleann Mhor* in July and August 1977. Small passenger launches also worked here including the *An Easdale*.

CUAN

Name	Built Acquired Disposed of Broken up	Cars (of average size) Hull type	Engine/ propulsion	Builder	Notes
Maid of Luing	1953 1953 1975 C1975	2 Wood	1 x 48 hp diesel Gardner engine. Single screw.	James Noble (Fraserburgh) Ltd	Displaced by *Belnahua* in 1972 but retained as spare vessel until 1975. Abandoned on the north shore of the nearby island of Shuna. Unique amongst turntables in that her wheelhouse was situated at the bow.
Belnahua	1972 1972 Still operational on route	6 Steel	2 x Diesel M6cy 262bhp 7.5 kn 2scr Type D11	Campbeltown Shipyard	Replaced the *Maid of Luing* on the crossing and still in service.

Also operating on this route is the *Torsa*, a passenger only vessel. When the *Belnahua* is away for overhaul, the *Grey Dog* acts as relief vessel. The *Grey Dog* is a cattle barge with a 3-car capacity. The turntable ferry *Glen Mallie* also deputised on the Cuan crossing, when she was employed at Glenelg, in 1978.

DORNIE

Name	Built Acquired Disposed of Broken up	Cars (of average size) Hull type	Engine/ propulsion	Builder	Notes
Un-named vessel	C1920 C1920 1950 C1950	1 Wood	Single Screw	Unknown	Only car ferry to operate at Dornie. Operated until a bridge opened in September 1940 between Ardelve and Dornie, but continued between Ardelve and Totaig until around 1950.

A flat bottomed barge which could carry a vehicle also worked here and was towed behind a small passenger launch.

KESSOCK

Name	Built Acquired Disposed of Broken up	Cars (of average size) Hull type	Engine/ propulsion	Builder	Notes
Lowestoft Belle	18xx 1921 1936 19xx	Carried a couple of vehicles if deck space was available. Steel.	Steam engined twin screw vessel.	Unknown	Originally a pleasure steamer along the Norfolk coast, she was introduced at Kessock in 1921. She could carry a couple of vehicles on the deck. Withdrawn from service in 1936.
Hope	1905 1939 1942 1947	1 Lorry or 3 small cars. Steel.	Compound steam engined screw vessel.	Mackay Brothers, Alloa	Previously a ferry on the Alloa crossing which was replaced by Kincardine bridge in 1936. Hastily purchased by the local authorities at Inverness after they took over the Kessock ferry in 1939 and placed on the route. Plagued with breakdowns and replaced by the St Mawes in 1942. Fate unknown.
St Mawes	1917 1942 1951 1951	5 on foredeck. Steel.	Steam engined screw.	Unknown	Built in 1917 and served as harbour launch for the Admiralty before being used on St Mawes to Falmouth ferry. Requisitioned by the Admiralty again in 1939 and used on Clyde before coming to Kessock in 1942. Broken up in 1951 after Eilean Dubh was introduced.
Eilean Dubh	1951 1951 1982 C2003	8 Steel	Twin Gleniffer diesels 2 x M4cy 160bhp 9kn 2scr. Replaced with Kelvins later in her career, then with Perkins when MacDonald Ferries purchased her.	James Lamont and Company Ltd, Port Glasgow	First purpose built car ferry on the Kessock crossing. Side loaded, although did have a turntable built in to the deck on board to aid manoeuvring vessels. Displaced by the Kessock bridge in 1982 and used by MacDonald ferries Ltd as a workboat until scrapped around 2003 at Invergordon.
Inbhir Nis	1953 1953 1967 C1972	4 Wood	2 x Gleniffer engines. Twin Screw.	James Noble (Fraserburgh) Ltd	Only dedicated turntable ferry at Kessock. Served until displaced by the Rosehaugh in 1967. Sold to Larne in 1969, Northern Ireland and then operated between Cromarty and Nigg between 1969 and 1972. Probably scrapped soon after.
Rosehaugh	1967 1967 1982 Still operational	17 Steel	Voith Schneider units.	Berwick Shipyard	Served at Kessock until bridge opened in 1982. Transferred to Corran. Displaced from Corran in 2001 by the arrival of the Corran. Currently owned by MacDonald Ferries, operating from Invergordon supplying oil rigs.

The Glenachulish also served here on relief between 1975 and 1982. Passenger vessels on this route included the Maid of Morven, Redcastle, Maud, Nellie, Ailsa and St Valery.

KYLEAKIN

Name	Built Acquired Disposed of Broken up	Cars (of average size) Hull type	Engine/ propulsion	Builder	Notes
Kyle	1917 1918 1938 C1940	1 Wood	1 x Kelvin Paraffin 2 cylinder. Single screw.	Bergius Company Ltd, Glasgow	First motor ferry on the Kyleakin crossing capable of conveying a vehicle. Had a car deck resembling a turntable but permanently fixed across the deck. Sold to David MacBrayne for use as a tender at Iona between 1938 and 1939. Then tender at Coll C1940. Fate unknown.
Skye	1922 1923 1950 Unknown	0 Wood	1 x Kelvin Paraffin 2 cylinder. Single screw.	James N Miller and Sons Ltd, St Monace	Passenger-only ferry used to supplement the sailings of the early vehicle ferries. Occasionally towed a barge capable of holding a vehicle. Sold in 1950 to Greenock for use as a pleasure launch.
Kyleakin (I)	1928 1928 1951 1959	1 (2 from 1931) Wood	1 x Kelvin Ricardo Petrol. Re-engined 1931. Single screw.	Webster and Bickerton Ltd, Goole	Re-engined and lengthened in 1931 to carry 2 cars . Served at Kyleakin until displaced by Lochalsh (I) and Portree (I). Sold for service at Glenelg.
Moil	1936 1936 1954 C1975	2 Wood	1 x 3 cylinder Gleniffer. Single screw.	Hugh McLean and Sons Ltd, Renfrew	Laid up as spare vessel at Kyleakin with the arrival of the Lochalsh (I) and Portree (I) in 1951. Retained as spare until 1954 when Broadford (I) arrived. Sold to British Transport Commission who used her as a workboat at Grangemouth. Transferred to the Forth in 1968. Fate unknown.
Cuillin	1942 1942 1954 C1965	2 Steel	1 x 3 cylinder Gleniffer. Single screw.	William Denny and Bros Ltd, Dumbarton	First steel hulled vessel on the Kyleakin route. Displaced by Broadford (I). Sold to John Lee, Belfast. Sold on to Newry Port and Harbour Trust and used as workboat. Still registered in 1965. Fate unknown.
Coruisk (I)	1947 1950 1954 C1959	0 Wood	2 x Perkins 6 cylinder diesel. Twin screw.	Yorkshire Yacht and Engineering Company Ltd, Bridlington	Built as Silver Grid in 1947. Arrived at Kyleakin in 1950. Passenger-only launch. Not needed after 1954 as Portree (I) and Broadford (I) had extensive passenger accommodation aft. Sold to H. Hilditch of Broadford. Destroyed by fire around 1959.
Lochalsh (I), Lochalsh II (I)	1951 1951 1958 C1995	2 Steel	1 x 4 cylinder Gleniffer. Single screw.	William Denny and Bros Ltd, Dumbarton	Laid up at Kyleakin in 1957 upon arrival of Lochalsh (II). Renamed Lochalsh II (I) to allow new vessel to use name. In 1958 she passed to BTC Waterways at Inverness at which time her turntable was removed and replaced by a small crane. She then passed to SeaBoard Marine and then McRae Marine at Nigg who used her in connection with the Nigg oil terminal and fish farming before laying her aside. The grounded vessel is still in existence at Nigg.
Portree (I), Portree II	1951 1952 1965 Still operational	4 Steel	2 x 4 cylinder Gleniffer. Twin screw.	William Denny and Bros Ltd, Dumbarton	Renamed Portree II to allow Portree (II) to be used by new vessel. Sold to Gerald Lee of Belfast in 1965. In 1967 sold to Orwell and Harwich Navigation Company then sold on to United Kingdom Atomic Energy Authority who made conversion to bow loading and placed her on private ferry in 1968 (until 1971) between Orford and Orford Ness. Since 2004 she has been working as a barge and dive vessel for Mojo Maritime based in Cornwall. Still operational as Portree II.

Broadford (I), Broadford II	1953 1954 1966 1981	4 Steel	2 x 4 cylinder Gleniffer. Twin screw.	William Denny and Bros Ltd, Dumbarton	Renamed *Broadford II* to allow *Broadford* (II) to be used by new vessel. Sold in January 1967 to the Orwell & Harwich Navigation Co Ltd, although they never moved her from Kyleakin. She remained at Kyleakin until March 1968 when she was sold to Marine Transport Ltd of Cobh, Ireland, eventually being scrapped in 1981.
Lochalsh (II), Lochalsh II (II)	1957 1957 1970 C1990	6 Steel	2 x 4 cylinder Gleniffer. Twin screw.	Ailsa Shipbuilding Company, Troon	Joint largest (in size, not capacity) turntable ever built (along with sister *Kyleakin* (II)). Laid up at Kyleakin upon arrival of *Kyleakin* (III). Chartered to David MacBrayne from April to October 1971 for use as Scalpay ferry then transferred to that company in December 1971. They renamed her *Scalpay* (II). Also served at Corran in 1977.
Kyleakin (II), Kyleakin II	1960 1960 1971 C1990	6 Steel	2 x 4 cylinder Gleniffer. Twin Screw.	Ailsa Shipbuilding Company, Troon	Joint largest (in size, not capacity) turntable ever built (along with sister *Lochalsh* (II)). Displaced from Kyleakin by arrival of *Lochalsh* (III). Operated relief at Scalpay in 1970 and was such a success the sister, *Lochalsh* (II) became permanent there. Converted to bow loading for use on Clyde and renamed *Largs* in June 1972. Operated from Largs to Cumbrae until sold to Ardmaleish shipyard in 1983. Laid up in Rothesay until sold to South Yemen in 1987. Fate unknown. She was distinguishable from her sister by their differing ramp mechanisms. *Kyleakin* (II)'s system pivoted on a horizontal 'J' shaped rail.
Portree (II)	1965 1965 1970 Still in existence	9 Steel	2 x 4 cylinder Gleniffer. Twin screw.	James Lamont and Company Ltd, Port Glasgow	Side-loading vessel built with wheelhouse forward. Displaced from Kyleakin by arrival of *Kyleakin* (III). Transferred to operate on Colintraive to Rhubodach route and converted to bow loading. Wheelhouse moved aft. Operated there from 1970 until 1986. Occasionally served as relief on Largs to Cumbrae route. Sold to Mr Hooper of Sandbank for supplying the US Navy submarine depots in the Holy Loch. Became a mooring in the Holy Loch and her hulk was still floating there in October 2011.
Broadford (II)	1966 1967 1971 C2005	9 Steel	2 x 4 cylinder Gleniffer. Twin screw.	James Lamont and Company Ltd, Port Glasgow	Side-loading vessel built with wheelhouse aft. Displaced from Kyleakin by arrival of *Lochalsh* (III). Transferred to operate on Colintraive to Rhubodach route and converted to bow loading. Operated there from 1971 until 1986. Occasionally served as relief on Largs to Cumbrae route. Sold to Mr Hooper of Sandbank for supplying the US Navy submarine depots in the Holy Loch. Sold to Divemex Ltd of Powys and renamed *Boreford*. Came back to Clyde in early 2000s renamed *Broadford Bay* and operated as a workboat. Scrapped around 2005.
Coruisk (II)	1969 1969 1971 C1995	9 Steel	2 x 4 cylinder English Electric Diesels (Kelvin). Twin screw.	Ailsa Shipbuilding Company, Troon	Side loading vessel built with wheelhouse aft. Displaced from Kyleakin by arrival of *Lochalsh* (III). Converted to bow loading and opened the Largs to Cumbrae service. Also served at Colintraive, Lismore, Mingary, Raasay and Scalpay. Sold in 1987 to a new owner in Penzance. Fate unknown.

Name	Built Acquired Disposed of Broken up	Cars (of average size) Hull type	Engine/ propulsion	Builder	Notes
Kyleakin (III)	1970 1970 1991 Still operational	28 Steel	2 x 8 cylinder Gardner. Voith Schneider units.	Newport Shipbuilding and Engineering Company Ltd, Newport	First drive through vessel on route. Served until the arrival of the *Loch Fyne* in 1991. Sold to United Marine Transport Services to operate a service across Cork Harbour. Renamed *Carrigaloe*.
Lochalsh (III)	1971 1971 1991 Still operational	28 Steel	2 x 8 cylinder Gardner. Voith Schneider units.	Newport Shipbuilding and Engineering Company Ltd, Newport	Second drive through vessel on the route. Served until the arrival of the *Loch Dunvegan* in 1991. Sold to United Marine Transport Services to operate a service across Cork Harbour. Renamed *Glenbrook*.
Loch Dunvegan (II)	1991 1991 1995 Still operational	36 Steel	2 x Volvo Penta marine engines. Voith Schneider units.	Ferguson Shipbuilders Ltd, Port Glasgow	One of the last pair of ferries on the Skye crossing. Laid up on the opening of the Skye bridge in 1995. Further use found and this vessel now mainly operates between Colintraive and Rhubodach. Also deputises on various other CalMac routes.
Loch Fyne	1991 1991 1995 Still operational	36 Steel	2 x Volvo Penta marine engines. Voith Schneider units.	Ferguson Shipbuilders Ltd, Port Glasgow	One of the last pair of ferries on the Skye crossing. Laid up on the opening of the Skye bridge in 1995. Further use found and this vessel now mainly operates between Lochaline and Fishnish. Also deputises on various other CalMac routes.

The *Glen Mallie* also relieved here in 1971 and 1972.

KYLERHEA

Name	Built Acquired Disposed of Broken up	Cars (of average size) Hull type	Engine/ propulsion	Builder	Notes
Kylerhea	C1935 1935 1951 C1960	2 Wood	1 x 28 hp petrol/ paraffin Kelvin. From 1959 1 x 4 cylinder Ailsa Craig diesel. Single screw.	Messrs Stevenson & Asher Boat builders, Banff	First motorised ferry at Glenelg. Did not operate during WW2. Ended up sunk at Inverie, Loch Nevis until raised and returned to route in 1959.
Kyleakin (I)	1928 1952 C1955 1959	2 Wood	1 x Kelvin Ricardo Petrol. Re-engined 1931. Single screw.	Webster and Bickerton Ltd, Goole	Served first at Kyleakin. Came to Glenelg in 1952 and operated by a Mr Forsythe. She was withdrawn prior to 1956 and later lost at Broadford during a storm in 1959.
Kylerhea	C1935 1959 1960 C1960	2 Wood	1 x 28 hp petrol paraffin Kelvin. From 1959 1 x 4 cylinder Ailsa Craig diesel. Single screw.	Messrs Stevenson & Asher Boat builders, Banff	Retrieved from Inverie, Loch Nevis and returned to route in 1959. Displaced by *Queen of Glen Albyn* in 1960. Fate unknown.
Queen of Glenalbyn	1936 1960 1961 C1964	2 Wood	1 x Gleniffer diesel. Single screw.	Messrs Stevenson & Asher Boat builders, Banff	Displaced from Ballchulish by the arrival of *Maid of Glencoe* (II) and *Glen Mallie*. Sold for use at Glenelg. Renamed *Queen of Glenalbyn*. Displaced from Glenelg by former Ballachulish fleet mate *Appin Chief*. Ended her days as a pontoon at Craignure for the building works of the new pier to accommodate the new car ferry service in 1964.

Appin Chief	1955 1961 C1971 C1975	4 Wood	1 x 4 cylinder Gleniffer diesel. Single screw.	James Noble (Fraserburgh) Ltd	Sold on for further service from Ballachulish. Joined by the *Glen Mallie* in 1969 but by 1971 only one boat was needed so *Appin Chief* was beached. She remained there for many years before being deliberately scuttled around 1988 in the Sound of Sleat. Also served at Scalpay on relief in 1968 and '69.
Glen Mallie	1959 1969 1982 C1985	6 Wood	1 x Gleniffer 4 cylinder diesel. Single screw.	James Noble (Fraserburgh) Ltd	Sold from Ballachulish for use at Glenelg in 1969. Served until 1982. Displaced by *Glenachulish* prior to start of season in 1983 and sold to Western Isles Islands Council. Used at Vatersay as a cattle barge and then abandoned on Vatersay in Cornaig Bay. Also served in relief capacity at Cuan in 1978, Scalpay in 1971, '72, '73, '74 and '75, as well as Kyle of Lochalsh in 1971 and '72.
Glenachulish	1969 1983 Still operational at Glenelg.	6 Steel	180 hp Kelvin T6. Single screw.	Ailsa Shipbuilding Company, Troon	Displaced from Ballachulish upon opening of bridge. Acquired by Highland Regional Council. Served as relief vessel at Corran, Kessock and Kylesku between 1975 and 1982 before being sold in 1983 for service at Glenelg. Between January and March 2012 she served at Strome due to a rockfall.

KYLESKU

Name	Built Acquired Disposed of Broken up	Cars (of average size) Hull type	Engine/ propulsion	Builder	Notes
Un-named bow loading vessel	C1920 C1920 C1950 C1950	1 Wood	Single screw.	Unknown	Commenced service soon after World War One had come to an end. It probably remained in service until *The Maid of Kylesku* entered service in the early 1950s. Fate unknown.
The Maid of Kylesku	1952 1952 1976 1976	4 Wood	1 x Kelvin diesel engine. Single screw.	James Noble (Fraserburgh) Ltd	Displaced by the *Queen of Kylesku* in 1967 but retained as spare vessel and for use at peak periods when a two-boat service was operated. Sold to local fisherman in 1976 after *Maid of Glencoul* had settled in. He reused the engines but left the hull to rot near her old crossing.
Mamore	1951 1959 1967 C1967	4 Wood	1 x 4 cylinder Gleniffer diesel. Single screw.	James Noble (Fraserburgh) Ltd	Displaced from Ballachulish by the *Glen Mallie* in 1959 and sold to Sutherland County Council for £1,200 who used her as a relief, and probably peak assistance, vessel on the crossing at Kylesku. After displacement by the *Queen of Kylesku* she was then sent to Lochinver to help with the construction of the pier extension there and then abandoned on the River Culag.
Queen of Kylesku	1967 1967 1984 C1990	9 small cars	Twin screw.	James Noble (Fraserburgh) Ltd	Displaced to spare vessel by *Maid of Glencoul* in 1975 but retained until the bridge opened in 1984. Sold and renamed *Queen of Tanera* and used at the Tanera More fish farm in the Summer Isles, Loch Broom. Abandoned on Tanera More where she still lies.
Maid of Glencoul	1975 1975 1984 Still operational	18 Steel	Twin Caterpillar diesel 2 x M6cy 500 bhp. Voith Schneider units.	MacCrindle Shipbuilding Ltd, Ardrossan	Displaced from Kylesku in 1984 after opening of bridge. Transferred to Corran where she is still operational.

The *Glenachulish* also served here on relief between 1975 and 1982. It is possible that the *Gleann Mhor* also served here on relief in 1983 and 1984.

SCALPAY

Name	Built Acquired Disposed of Broken up	Cars (of average size) Hull type	Engine/ propulsion	Builder	Notes
Scalpay (I) (ex Maid of Glencoe (II))	1956 1965 1971 1971	4 Wood	1 x 4 cylinder Gleniffer. Re-engined late1958 with 1 x Kelvin, replaced later by 1 x 4 cylinder Gleniffer. Single screw.	James Noble (Fraserburgh) Ltd	Displaced from Ballchulish by the *Glen Loy*. Sold to David MacBrayne who renamed her *Scalpay* (I). Inaugurated new service across Kyles Scalpay. Displaced by *Scalpay* (II), ex *Lochalsh* (II) after she was condemned structurally and mechanically at quinquennial survey on Gareloch. She was acquired by Timbercraft Ltd who scrapped the engines and used the hull as a pontoon.
Scalpay (II) (ex Lochalsh II (II))	1957 1971 1977 C1990	6 Steel	2 x 4 cylinder Gleniffer. Twin screw.	Ailsa Shipbuilding Co. Ltd, Troon	Displaced from Kyleakin upon arrival of *Kyleakin* (III). Chartered to David MacBrayne from April to October 1971 for use as Scalpay ferry then transferred to that company in December 1971 and renamed *Scalpay* (II). Also in October angles cut into ramps to aid loading at the narrow slipways either side of Kyles Scalpay. Replaced *Scalpay* (I) on the route and served until 1977. Covered *Gleann Mhor* at Corran in 1977 then laid up at Lochaline and Shandon. Purchased by Ardmaleish shipyard for £200 who berthed her at Rothesay and used her for spares. She lost her deck structures by 1983 and eventually became a barge along the Ayrshire coast and was probably abandoned in the late 1980s.
Morvern	1972 1977 1977 Still operational	5 Steel	2 x 6 cylinder Kelvin. Twin screw.	James Lamont & Co. Ltd, Port Glasgow	The first bow loader on the Scalpay crossing started on the 13th January 1977.She first operated 6 sailings a day to Tarbert, but from the 16th May she could use the enlarged slipways each side of the Kyles. She handed over to *Kilbrannan* on the 2nd June. Now operates in Ireland from Castletownbere to Bere Island.
Kilbrannan	1972 1977 1990 Still operational.	5 Steel	2 x 6 cylinder Kelvin. Twin screw.	James Lamont & Co. Ltd, Port Glasgow	First of the CalMac 'Island' class boats. Served throughout the MacBrayne network. Became Scalpay ferry after withdrawal of *Scalpay* (II). Sold out of fleet in 1992 but has served in Ireland since then. Currently serves Clare Island as *Clew Bay Queen*.
Canna	1975 1990 1997 Still operational.	6 Steel	2 x Scania D9 93M35 turbo-charged 6 cylinder diesels. Twin screw.	James Lamont & Co. Ltd, Port Glasgow	Another CalMac bow loading 'Island' class vessel. Served Scalpay for 7 years. Now operates from Ballycastle to Rathlin Island in Northern Ireland. Still named *Canna*.
Rhum	1972 1997 1997 Still operational.	6 Steel	2 x 6 cylinder Kelvin. Twin screw.	James Lamont & Co. Ltd, Port Glasgow	One of CalMac's bow loading 'Island' class ferries. Final ferry to serve Scalpay before bridge opened in 1997. Currently serves Arranmore Island in Ireland. Still named *Rhum*.

Various turntable vessels operated here on relief. The *Appin Chief* in 1968 and '69, *Kyleakin* (II) in 1970 and *Glen Mallie* in 1971, '72, '73, '74 and '75. Other members of the 'Island' class bow loading vessels also served as well as former Kyleakin vessel *Coruisk* (II).

STROME

Name	Built Acquired Disposed of Broken up	Cars (of average size) Hull type	Engine/ propulsion	Builder	Notes
Un-named turntable vessel (May have been named *Maid of Strome*)	C1920 C1920 C1959 C1959	1 bus or 2 small cars Wood	Single screw.	Unknown	First motorised car ferry at Strome. Joined by *Highland Queen* and probably retained as spare vessel. Probably withdrawn after both 2 car ferries were introduced.
Highland Queen	1938 1938 C1962 C1962	2 Wood	Single screw.	Unknown	Operated the Strome crossing until joined by *Strome Castle* in 1959. Probably retained until 1962 when *Pride of Strome* was introduced. Vessel laid aside at South Strome.
Strome Castle (I)	C1940 C1940 C1962 C1970	2 Wood	Single screw.	Unknown	Second 2-car ferry which operated alongside *Highland Queen*. When displaced she was used as a dive boat, with a cabin added where the turntable was. Laid aside at North Strome.
Strome Castle (II)	1958 1959 1970 1970	6 Wood	1 x Gleniffer. Single screw.	James Noble (Fraserburgh) Ltd	Penultimate ferry on the Strome crossing. Laid up at Stromeferry after bypass opened. She still languishes on Loch Carron
Pride of Strome	1962 1962 1970 1970	6 (maybe more at a squeeze)	2 x Gleniffer. Twin screw.	Forbes of Sandhaven	Very well equipped vessel - twin screw and oak hulled. Very short career ended when laid up at Stromeferry after bypass opened. She still languishes on Loch Carron.
Glenachulish†	1969 2012 2012 Still Operational	6 Steel	180 hp Kelvin T6. Single screw.	Ailsa Shipbuilding Company, Troon	Due to a rockfall on the main road from Dingwall to Plockton, the *Glenachulish* and passenger craft *Sula Mhor* operated an emergency ferry service at Strome between January and March 2012. *Glenachulish* has also served at Ballachulish, Corran, Kessock, Kylesku and Glenelg.
Sula Mhor†	1950 2012 2012 Still operational	0 Wood	2 x Ford V8 engines with 120 horse power. Twin Screw.	Cooks Yard, River Blackwater, Essex	Built for service in 1950. Served on St Mawes ferry, Cornwall, as *New Princess Maud*. Came to Scotland in 2006 and to Plockton in 2009.

Due to a rockfall on the main road from Dingwall to Plockton, the *Glenachulish* and *Sula Mhor* operated an emergency ferry service at Strome between January and March 2012. Usually offers seal trips from Plockton.
† means the vessels only served in an emergency capacity in 2012.

Far left: *The Maid of Kylesku* is seen during 1964 . (David Yates)

Left: The **Glen Duror** at South Ballachulish.

BIBLIOGRAPHY

Neil King's blog- 'Except the Kyles and Western Isles'

Last Ferry to Skye – Christopher J Uncles

Caledonian Steam Packet - Iain C. MacArthur

Various Clyde River Steamer Club Reviews

A Celebration of the Kessock Ferries – North Kessock and District Local History Society

Wheels around Lochaber – Robert Grieves

Wheels around Skye and Lochalsh – Robert Grieves

Ferry Tales of Argyll and the Isles – Walter Weyndling

Ferries of Scotland – Marie Weir

Royal Road to the Isles – Ian McCrorie

'Cruising Monthly' – the newsletter of the Coastal Cruising Association

Google news archives of the 'Glasgow Herald' and 'The Bulletin'

ACKNOWLEDGEMENTS

A huge word of thanks to the Rt. Hon. Alex Salmond PC MSP, First Minister of Scotland, for agreeing to provide the Foreword to this publication.

The authors also express their sincere gratitude to award winning Scottish journalist John MacLeod for his interest, support and encouragement throughout the process of compiling this book and also for providing his excellent Introduction.

Thanks also to Clive Pearson (CEO of the Isle of Skye CIC), Dr Jennifer Frances (*Glenachulish* Preservation Trust), Chris Reid (Fraserburgh Heritage Society), Donald Kennedy (Loch Etive Cruises), Donald Kennedy (former skipper of the *Dhuirnish*), Bill Leech (Oban War & Peace Museum), Walter Cumming (North Kessock & District Local History Society), Jamie Gaukroger (Am Baile Support), Richard Stenlake (Stenlake Publishing), Dr Colin Smith, Ian Hall, Anna Belle (Kyleakin History Society), Dr Bruce Peter (AE Glen collection), Brian Maxted, David Parsons, John Newth, Steven Munro (skipper of the *Corran*), Angus Mackinnon, Simon Thomson, Kathryn Preston (GL Watson & Co Ltd), Elspeth Reid (Falkirk Museums), Neil King, Tim Aymes (Scottish Motor Museum Trust), Dr Jim Mackay and Gavin Meldrum (Kirkmichael Trust),

Finally grateful thanks go to all those people who have kindly submitted photographic images for inclusion in this book. Their work is credited elsewhere and the book would have certainly been the poorer without their timely and welcome contributions. All uncredited photographs are from Robert Beale's collection.

The twilight of the turntable ferry at South Ballachulish as the *Glenachulish* (left) and the *Glen Duror* (off service) lie under the shadow of the new bridge. (*Gregory Melle*)